Scotland and the United Kingdom

This study explores the economic case for Scotland's continued union with the UK.

The growth of political support for the Scottish National Party during the past twenty years has generated substantial debate in Scotland about the relative virtues of independence or continued union with the United Kingdom. The exploitation of 'Scotland's oil' from the 1970s provided an economic basis for the case for independence. This book explores the case for union, devolution or independence on economic grounds.

Professor Lee surveys the economic transition of the Scottish economy during the twentieth century in which much established heavy industry declined, leaving a legacy of unemployment and poverty for which new industries were unable fully to compensate. These severe economic problems – especially concentrated in central Scotland – focused attention on the role of the state in running the economy, particularly as such intervention greatly increased in the twentieth century. Government intervention has been influential through substantial increases in both taxation and public expenditure, as well as through regional and industrial policy.

C. H. Lee is Professor of Economics at the University of Aberdeen.

Insights from Economic History
General editor: Nick Crafts

This series makes accessible major results from recent research in economic history, with an emphasis on issues of current importance. The books present an authoritative and objective view of the 'lessons of history' for the non-expert, while comprising essential reference material for the professional economic historian. The focus of the series is on issues in economic history that have contemporary relevance for policy makers and for economists wishing for a digest of key research results.

Also in this series

Barry Eichengreen
Reconstructing Europe's trade and payments: the European Payments Union

Forrest Capie
Tariffs and growth: some insights from the world economy, 1850–1940

Clive Lee

Scotland and the United Kingdom

The economy and the Union in the twentieth century

Manchester University Press

Manchester and New York

Distributed exclusively in the USA and Canada by St Martin's Press

Copyright © Clive Lee 1995

Published by Manchester University Press
Oxford Road, Manchester M13 9NR, UK
and Room 400, 175 Fifth Avenue, New York, NY 10010, USA

Distributed exclusively in the USA and Canada
by St Martin's Press, Inc., 175 Fifth Avenue, New York, NY 10010, USA

British Library Cataloguing-in-Publication Data
A catalogue record for this book is available from the British Library

Library of Congress Cataloging-in-Publication Data
Lee, C. H. (Clive Howard). 1942–
    Scotland and the United Kingdom: the economy and the Union in the twentieth
century / Clive Lee.
        p.   cm. — (Insights from economic history)
    Includes bibliographical references.
    ISBN 0–7190–4100–7 (hbk). — ISBN 0–7190–4101–5 (pbk).
    1. Scotland—Economic conditions. 2. Great Britain—Economic conditions.
3. Great Britain—Economic policy. I. Title. II. Series.
HC257.S4L383   1995
330.9411'082—dc20   95–5482
                                                                                CIP

ISBN 0 7190 4100 7 *hardback*
     0 7190 4101 5 *paperback*

First published 1995

99 98 97 96 95   10 9 8 7 6 5 4 3 2 1

Typeset in Great Britain
by Northern Phototypesetting Co Ltd, Bolton
Printed in Great Britain
by Biddles Ltd, Guildford and King's Lynn

Contents

Figures and tables

Figures

Tables

For Bertie, Eddie, Johnny, Kathleen and Martin

Acknowledgements

It is invariably true that the writer of any study such as this incurs a large number of debts to others. Earlier versions of this book were read in draft form by several friends and scholars. The present version is much improved by their efforts although, sadly, the author still has to accept final responsibility. But I would like to express my great thanks to Roy Campbell, Nick Crafts, Francis Brooke, David Newlands and Peter Wardley. I would also like to thank Kevin Pringle, Research Officer of the Scottish National Party for providing me with various documents, in spite of the fact that he was once a student of mine.

Part I

Introduction

Chapter 1

The history of the Union: politics and economics

The parliaments of England and Scotland were joined in the Treaty of Union which came into effect in May 1707, just over a century after the crowns of the two countries had been united in the person of James I and VI in 1603. This Union created a single British legislature at Westminster. The new House of Commons included 45 Scottish members in a total of 558, and the English House of Lords acquired 16 Scottish peers, while the Scottish legislature in Edinburgh ceased to exist. The Union did not establish a complete merger of the two states. Scotland retained its separate Church and legal system. But in economic affairs the Union was complete as customs barriers were dismantled and the new unified state had a single currency, a single system of taxation, and a common economic policy. Indeed 15 of the 25 articles in the Treaty of Union were concerned with economic matters.

The new state did not come into existence without considerable dispute, mainly within Scotland, and such debate has continued with varying intensity through the period of almost three hundred years since its inception. The increase in Scottish dissatisfaction in recent decades, as manifest in the growth of popular support for the Scottish National Party, has stimulated interest in the Union and the gains and losses attributed to it. This analysis is concerned solely with the economic aspects of that debate. It is, of course, true that some would support the Union even if there were a clear and substantial economic cost, while others would reject it however great the economic benefit. Nevertheless the economic dimension represents an important aspect of the larger question, and is one of the issues which have been debated vigorously for three centuries.

The politics of union

There has been much discussion about the motives and aspirations of the two parties who created the new state. There is general agreement about the English aim which stemmed from the increasing strain between a unified crown and two sovereign states which emerged during the course of the seventeenth century, and particularly the fear that an independent Scotland would refuse to provide support for an English war. As a diplomatic observer noted at the union of the crowns: 'England hath gotten no great catch by the addition of Scotland; she had only got a wolf by the ears, who must be held very fast, else he will run away to France' (Levack 1987: 217). England wanted political and diplomatic security and the Treaty of Union offered, and indeed secured, that prize. Having thus realised their principal objective, the English have taken little apparent interest in the Union since 1707 other than to observe, with some perplexity, the heat of debate in the north.

Far more acrimonious argument has centred on the aims of the Scots in signing the treaty, and whether any but a few citizens of that country actually supported it. Political historians have argued that an unpopular treaty was forced through the division lobby by political management aided by bribery and the divisions within an ineffective opposition. Such views reiterate a view popular in the nineteenth century that 'The Union was, in fact, carried by the Parliament, with the assistance of the Church, against the country'(Ferguson 1977: 266–7).

There were manifestations of discontent in Scotland in the first half of the eighteenth century followed by a century of quiet. But elements of discontent with the Union reappeared in the middle of the nineteenth century. In 1853 a National Association for the Vindication of Scottish Rights was formed with the support of political and professional groups with the aim of securing increased representation at Westminster and a secretary of state devoted to Scottish affairs. Public meetings drew 5,000 people in Glasgow and 2,000 in Edinburgh but the association was disbanded after only three years. A Secretary for Scotland was eventually appointed in 1885 in response to political pressure, establishing a trend of devolution by concession. The issue of home rule was certainly debated in the later decades of the century although it was clearly overshadowed by the Irish question. But the Conservative Party in office was easily able to defeat the resolutions which were put forward and the Liberals did not advance the cause of Scottish home rule during their term of office in the 1890s. The establishment of the naval base at Rosyth and the army barracks at Stobs were, it has been claimed, the main gains from devolution (Donaldson 1969: 10).

The twentieth century brought a significant increase in political activity aimed at securing home rule for Scotland. In 1924 the Scottish Liberal Party adopted the cause although, by then, its influence was waning. A Home Rule Association was formed in 1917 which devised a bill to abandon Scottish representation at Westminster in exchange for dominion status. The decline of the Liberals meant a similar decline in parliamentary support for home rule, but the devolutionary trend continued as the Secretary for Scotland was upgraded to Secretary of State in 1926 and Scottish administration was moved to St Andews House in Edinburgh in the 1930s.

Pressure for independence was manifest in the formation of new political parties. In 1928 the National Party of Scotland, with a left wing bias, was formed to secure complete separation from the United Kingdom. A more moderate Scottish Party was formed in 1932, and these two parties amalgamated in 1934 to form the Scottish National Party. This party also split in 1942, as some moderates left to form the Scottish Convention. This body produced a National Covenant at the end of the 1940s, pledged to secure a Scottish parliament within the framework of the United Kingdom (Donaldson 1969: 14). But until the 1970s the nationalists received poor support at the ballot box, winning seats only at by-elections at Motherwell in 1945 and Hamilton in 1967. The nationalists were confined to 1 per cent of the Scottish popular vote in the 1930s and rather less than that in the 1950s (Cornford and Brand 1969: 35). The 5 per cent share of the vote secured in 1966 marked a large improvement in the fortunes of the SNP. Membership increased sharply at the end of the decade and the party secured a record 30.4 per cent of the Scottish vote at the General Election in October 1974. This marked a high point as the party secured seven and eleven MPs respectively in the two elections of that year. In subsequent general elections support for the SNP has varied between 11.8 per cent and 17.3 per cent in 1979, 1983 and 1987 before rising to 24.0 per cent in 1992. But on each of these occasions the popular vote was only translated into two or three MPs (Craig 1989: 95). The SNP thus advanced from being a political fringe organisation in the 1950s to become a serious political force, although it remained well short of the scale of support needed to provide a mandate to negotiate independence. The 1979 referendum on devolution reflected the wide diversity of support for different options: 32.9 per cent of voters were in favour, 30.8 per cent were against and 36.3 per cent were, implicitly, indifferent in that they failed to vote.

But another element of the political equation fuelled Scottish discontent in the 1980s and 1990s. As the vagaries of the electoral system returned a Conservative administration with a large overall majority of seats in the House of Commons but with only about 43 per cent of the popular vote at each of the general elections between 1979 and 1992, Conservative support fell sharply in Scotland. In 1970 the Conservatives secured 38.0 per cent of the Scottish vote. By 1979 this had fallen to 31.4 per cent and by 1987 and 1992 was less than 25 per cent (Craig 1989: 41–9). The regional polarisation of political support created a situation in which the national government could claim a United Kingdom mandate for its policies while enjoying the support of only one quarter of Scottish voters. Throughout the 1980s there was little popular support and much popular hostility towards the radical conservative policies emanating from the Scottish Office in Edinburgh.

The economics of Union

Economic matters have played a much larger part in debates about Scotland and the Union than they have in England. This includes both the original motivation for joining the Union and the subsequent effects of that decision. The gloomiest version of the economic thesis depicts early eighteenth-century Scotland as a backward and impoverished state whose only chance of rescue from enduring stagnation lay in joining with a larger and more affluent partner in what has been termed the largest common market in Europe at the time. This version puts great emphasis on the Darien failure. This was a scheme launched in 1695 by London based Scottish merchants to establish a Scottish trading colony in Africa and the Indies similar to the English East India Company in order to provide markets for Scottish manufactures. English pressure ensured that capital for the venture could not be obtained in London or Amsterdam, the two principal financial centres in Europe. Eventually the new company established a single colony at Darien in Central America, although it was soon driven out by the Spanish colonial government whose territory had been appropriated. The scheme was not only a total failure but absorbed an estimated 25 per cent of all Scottish liquid trading assets. Its collapse in 1700, set against several years of poor harvests, meant that 'when contemporaries at the turn of the century observed the falling volumes of overseas trade, the widespread vagrancy and unemployment, and the national exchequer practically empty of funds, it seemed to them that Scotland was on the verge of economic collapse' (Smout 1964: 459).

Supporting such an interpretation, or a modified version of it, is the fact that in the late seventeenth century, the English market was becoming increasingly important for Scottish traders while trade relations became more difficult. As the seventeenth century progressed an increasing share of Scottish exports appear to have been destined for England, so that half the total were sold there by the end of the century. Further, in the commercial crises of 1667, 1681 and 1689, the Scots had made overtures with regard to a 'union of traid' to secure access to the English market without the obstacles of tariff barriers. In the 1690s tariffs on Scottish linen were increased by the English and new tariffs imposed on coal and salt. The English government increased pressure for union by threatening further economic sanctions. The Alien Act of 1705 stated that unless the Scots appointed commissioners to negotiate such a treaty, all Scots would be regarded as aliens in England, estates owned in that country would be confiscated, and Scottish cattle, linen and coal would be totally excluded from its markets. Since cattle comprised some 40 per cent of Scottish exports to England, and underpinned the balance of trade, the threat to the impoverished Scottish exchequer was severe. Indeed the Scottish state finances were in such a poor condition in 1707 that there was insufficient revenue to pay the army and the civil establishment. One historian concluded: 'As the Scottish parliament had little option but to surrender to what was in effect economic blackmail, it does not seem surprising that these issues did not dominate negotiations. There was nothing to discuss; continued trade to England in the key commodities of linen and black cattle was assured as long as the Scots played ball' (Whatley 1989: 151).

Recently, Devine has sought to modify this version of events by advancing the case that pre-Union Scotland was not without some capacity for economic growth and that the expansion achieved in the eighteenth century was, therefore, partly inherent in Scottish society. Given the predominance of agriculture in the early modern economy, this sector was crucial for the performance of the entire economy. Since Scottish agriculture was well able to feed the population dependent on it, and generate a surplus for export in the late seventeenth century, it cannot be regarded as inert or irredeemably backward. He identified several elements of agricultural advance in a shift towards single and larger tenancies in parts of the Lowlands, an increase in the length and formalisation of leases, conversion of rentals from payment in kind to payment in money, and some modest productivity increase through enclosure and improved rotation (Devine 1985: 26). All this, he argued, reflected the organic evolution of the agricultural sector apart from any political or trade regime.

Devine amplified this thesis of moderate but inherent growth in seventeenth-century Scotland by reference to the changing pattern of trade away from traditional European markets and towards England, so that half Scottish trade lay with her southern neighbour by 1700. Further, this slow change was accompanied and assisted by a change in the attitude of the Scottish ruling classes which perceived economic advance as being in their personal and collective interest. 'For the first time, between 1660 and 1700, an increase in national economic power became the aim both of Scottish government and the landed elite which it represented' (Devine 1985: 27).

There is no doubt that these arguments provide a salutary rebuttal to the simplistic notions that the Scottish economy was backward beyond redemption without the stimulus of the Union. But the points raised provide support for the rationality of entering the Union on economic grounds. The opportunities both for expanding trade and improving estates to benefit from that trade were far greater, and consistent with the pattern of development Devine describes, within the Union than outside it. As has been noted by many historians, Scottish landowners were increasingly aware that the revenue from their estates did not support the lifestyle of the London society they wished to enjoy.

The economic case for entering the Union can, of course, be expressed in considerably more positive terms. Such a perspective usually emphasises the gains to be obtained through access to larger markets on favourable terms, both the English domestic market and the extensive English colonial territories. The Scots traded with the latter before 1707 illegally, but the risks and costs of smuggling precluded any large scale venture and proscribed profits. The only way in which the obstacles imposed by the Navigation Acts, which limited trade with the colonies to English traders in English vessels, could be overcome on any significant scale was through the Union.

Some historians have accepted the overwhelming economic advantage of the Union for Scotland as a prime reason for signing the treaty, either as an escape from poverty or a most lucrative opportunity, and Marxist historians have argued that the combined gain of augmented accumulation from export trade and military protection for colonial ventures made the Union a logical choice for the Scottish ruling and commercial classes.

But not all sections of Scottish society perceived an economic gain. The town of Stirling petitioned against the Union citing the 'Insupportable burden of Taxation (which) all the grant of freedome of Trade will never Counterballance' (Whatley 1989: 156–7). Popular discontent reflected fears about unemployment and the prospect of hefty taxation on malt, ale and salt imposed by the highly efficient English revenue authorities. Indeed some of the opposition to Union was based on the fear of an efficient tax regime being introduced. Some industrialists feared they would lose the home market, on which they relied, to English imports. The salt industry sold its entire output in Scotland, while the coal mines on the Forth sold twice as much to the local saltpans as they exported to the south.

None of the views about the primacy of economic or political motivations for the Union are necessarily mutually exclusive, as indicated in a recent review of the historiographical debate (Whatley 1994). The political explanations doubtless reflect the way in which the treaty was managed through the political process. But it seems unlikely that economic consid- erations were without significance. That the balance of eco- nomic opportunity and threat favoured the Union, especially amongst those with wealth and political influence, seems likely and does not imply, as some have thought, a reliance on eco- nomic determinism. Smout's conclusion that the Union appeared to offer Scotland the best way out of economic reces- sion does seem to stand the test of time better than the more doctrinaire alternatives.

The economic effects of Union

There has been considerable debate about the economic effects of the Union especially in the context of the century following 1707. There has been general agreement that Scotland did not experience great gain or loss in the short run. Some early crit- ics emphasised the imposition or increase of taxes on linen, salt and malt, and the subjection to a far more efficient cus- toms service which was inimical to the smuggling industry. But it has been estimated that in the half century after 1707, while the bulk of the revenue raised in Scotland came from land and malt taxes, only some 15–20 per cent of that revenue was despatched to the Exchequer in London. There were benefits from tariffs, the linen industry gaining from protection against highly competitive German and Dutch imports as well as from a bounty on exports. Scotland also received fiscal compensa- tion for undertaking a share of the national debt which Eng- land had accumulated. The Equivalent was a capitalised valuation of the existing revenue yield and comprised a trans- fer of £398,085 to Scotland at the time of the Union. A second

payment, an 'Arising Equivalent', was to be a continuing compensation paid from revenue raised in Scotland and equal to
the entire increase in the customs and excise revenue in Scotland during the seven years following union. Expenditure from
these sources was to be devoted to paying the Scottish national
debt, compensation for those who lost through standardisa-
tion of the coinage or the Darien venture, plus financial assistance to economic development projects. Gains from this
financial source were disappointing for the Scots as the revenue returns were rather weak and the demands of Scottish
aristocrats and officials drained the fund. Perhaps the most
substantive gain from this transfer of funds came from the
activites of the Board of Trustees for Manufactures and Fish-
eries which was established in 1727 to administer the revenue
provided by the Equivalent for economic development. It also
received any surplus from the malt tax above £20,000 as an
additional regular income. The Board was most influential in
enouraging improvements in the linen industry, supporting
attempts to obtain better flax and advocating the need for
better bleaching of the finished cloth (Campbell 1964: 473–6).

While the short-term economic effects of the Union were
disappointing to some Scots, historians have generally agreed
that in the longer term Scotland gained substantially from it.
The principal effects on an economy joining a customs union
or common market, and the Treaty of Union effectively created both, are found in changes in trade and the balance of
payments. The crucial feature of such organisations is that
there are no trade restrictions between members while the
internal market is protected by a unified external tariff. Thus
Scotland gained privileged access to the English mainland and
colonial markets. There is no doubt that, in the medium term
if not immediately, this provided a considerable advantage for

the Scottish economy.

Historians have generally assumed, and the evidence has corroborated this, that the flow of trade went primarily from north to south, and in the form of black cattle and linen. This was Adam Smith's view and, in his judgement, comprised the main Scottish gain from the Union. While one estimate for 1701 suggested that 14,000 cattle were sent to the English market, by the 1720s some 30,000 were sold annually at the great market at Crieff before heading south. In the boom created by the Napoleonic Wars at the end of the century some 100,000 cattle per annum followed the same route across the border, although 80,000 per annum had been reached by mid century (Whatley 1989: 176). Adam Smith thought the trade could have been even greater had Scots been able to afford to improve their land and buy a greater stock of cattle for rearing.

More than access to the English market, historians have stressed the advantage to Scotland of securing access to the English colonies, free from the harassments of the hitherto covert smuggling trade. This was a great benefit to the west of Scotland, especially to Glasgow, whose merchants flourished in the eighteenth century Atlantic trade. By 1775 Scottish tobacco imports, some of which were re-exported to the European mainland, reached 45 million lbs and had formed the basis for several fortunes. By this date tobacco comprised 38 per cent of Scottish imports and 56 per cent of exports. 'The reward for the successful was wealth on a scale never before imagined in Scotland … Such riches quickly changed the face of Glasgow. The merchants' town house dominated the burgh while the rise of the luxury trades was another consequence of their achievement' (Devine 1975: 161–71). In addition, the chronicler of the tobacco trade enumerates multiplier effects in the growth of urban expansion, partly funded by the merchants, and the growth of a commercial infrastructure of banks, insurance companies and dockyards.

The linen industry also gained from access to colonial markets, further aided by the introduction of an export subsidy in 1743. Linens exported from Scotland increased from 1.85 million yards in the 1760s to 6.99 million in the 1790s, a very large share of which went to North America and the West Indies. Not only were export markets vital to this industry, but in the eighteenth century helped by government policy, it was gradually able to restrict foreign linens to an ever-declining share of the home and export markets, and more than hold its own against Irish competition (Durie 1979: 152–3).

A common market is also characterised by the free movement of capital and labour within its boundaries. The steady flow of Scots to the south has been a feature of the three centuries since the formation of the Union with much smaller numbers of United Kingdom citizens moving in the opposite direction, a fact which appears to have escaped the notice of contemporary organisations such as Settler Watch, raising the spectre of incomers taking jobs and homes from indigenous Scots. Capital almost certainly moved in both directions, although it is harder to delineate and impossible to quantify. Campbell speculated that the Union might have increased a destabilising flow of capital weakening the Scottish balance of payments, although the improved trade from the colonial markets in mid century would have been an effective corrective force (Campbell 1974: 60–4).

The effects of such changes in the patterns of trade and the allocation of productive factors has significant effects on welfare. Theory suggests that while there will be a net gain in welfare to the customs union as a whole there will be gains and losses sustained by specific groups in each of the countries comprising the new trading body. For individual countries there may be a net gain or loss. In the context of 1707 Scotland's relative poverty provided some insulation against the possibility of loss through the domestic market being flooded by English goods because many commodities were beyond the pockets of most citizens. Cattle traders certainly gained. Those whose activities were usually pursued away from the gaze of the revenue authorities probably lost. In the longer run, and certainly through the imperial heyday from the mid eighteenth century to 1914, the Scots almost certainly gained.

The final implication of a common market with a single currency is that it diminishes the scope for adopting monetary flexibility as a means of dealing with balance of payments difficulties. Scotland thus became tied to the monetary policies of the Bank of England and lost the capacity to unilaterally devalue the currency to boost exports. Until the present century, this was probably not a particularly significant problem. On the other hand, the greater price stability which should obtain under such a regime will generate benefits in increased market efficiency.

There is little doubt that historians will continue to debate the reasons for the formation of the Union, at least from the Scottish perspective. But there seems little doubt that, from an exclusively economic viewpoint, and in the longer term, the Union was a great success. It facilitated the growth inherent in the Scottish economy and provided a far more stimulating and extended environment for that growth in the eighteenth century than would have been possible otherwise. Whatever the true motivation which caused the Scots to join the Union it was by far the best possible economic policy available to them.

The economics of the Union were little discussed by contemporaries through the nineteenth century, nor has the subject attracted the interest of historians. In the period of economic expansion, imperial growth and early industrialisation which is usually characterised as the years from the mid eighteenth century to the First World War, Scotland experienced a structural transformation and economic growth similar in type and scale to the rest of the United Kingdom. Thus shipbuilding on Clydeside mirrored the same industry on the Tyne and Wear, mining in Central Scotland had its counterparts in South Wales, Durham and Yorkshire, Glasgow was a centre of engineering like London and the Midlands, and the Edinburgh financial sector mirrored the City of London. The economics of the Union had created a seamless industrial and financial web.

Economic decline and political discontent

The political discontent with the Union which grew in Scotland after the First World War was certainly linked to changing economic circumstances. Prior to 1914 Scottish national identity had been based on the notion of partnership with England in founding and running the Empire. Glasgow boasted that it was the second city of the Empire as Clyde-built ships provided a visible contribution to imperial trade, and other aspects of imperial expansion gave Scots the opportunity to pursue careers and glory as explorers, soldiers, diplomats or missionaries. The decline of the Empire and economic difficulties in the twentieth century necessitated the reformulation of that national identity, while growing unemployment emphasised economic difficulties. In the 1920s the Scots National League argued that economic and social problems were the result of poor government from Westminster and produced

highly dubious statistics to suggests that Scots were heavily
overtaxed while receiving none of the benefits of government
spending (Finlay 1994a: 61). Railway and bank amalgamations
in the 1920s which saw control pass away from Scotland articulated the threat that Scotland would become economically
marginalised, and that industry would be sucked away from
Scotland leaving depopulation and deindustrialisation. In 1932
The Scotsman newspaper complained that economic rationalisation would reduce Scotland to a mere province of England,
while the President of the Edinburgh Chamber of Commerce
complained that 'Business after business was being bought up
by English money and factories one after another closed down
... if the process of English absorption is not stopped, Scotland
will drop to a position of industrial insignificance' (Finlay
1994b: 10).

The economic problems which gave rise to the political discontent which has grown throughout the century provide the
essential background against which the economic virtues of
the Union must be evaluated. Without such economic problems it is, of course, possible that the Union would still have
been questioned and challenged. But the nature of that attack
would have been very different. For that reason, the first half
of this study explores the nature of the economic transition
which Scotland, like many other parts of the industrialised
world, has experienced throughout this century.

The context of massive structural transformation in which
apparently secure industries declined and created a flood of
unemployment, and in which poverty and urban decay compounded the problems of economic regeneration, is important
for two principal reasons. Firstly, because it reflects the cause
of much discontent and, secondly, because the role of the state
in economic management has become much greater and more

obviously intrusive in the twentieth century, thus making it an easy focus for blame. Painful economic adjustment and government economic management have been two of the major influences on the twentieth century history of all industrial countries. Their conjunction in the experience of Scotland explains why so much attention has become concentrated on the most obvious manifestation of them both, the Union itself.

Part II

The economics of structural change

Chapter 2

The Victorian legacy

The economics of Union

For almost three hundred years Scotland has been part of the Union with England. The economic impact of that Union on its constituent members can only be measured by calculating the difference between the actual performance of the economies involved and their performance in the context of the most probable alternative scenario had the Union not been established. This raises, of course, very great difficulties of estimation such that any resultant conclusion is likely to be regarded with some reservation by most observers. In defence of such speculation, it should be pointed out that this is the only means by which direct comparisons can be made and that, in reality, the alternatives to union were not infinite in number. It is not proposed here to offer detailed or quantified hypothetical models, but to make some suggestions about the most probable economic effects which might have been experienced had Scotland remained independent after 1707.

In principle, the various effects of joining or not joining such a union are well known and are very similar to those entailed when the United Kingdom debated and eventually joined the European Community in 1973. The merging of separate economies into a customs union removes all artificial restraints on trade, such as tariffs or quotas, so that trade between them is determined by market forces. The formation of a common market allows the free movement of labour and capital between the member states. Apart from trade and factor mobility, the main effect of such an economic merger is the impact of policy which is now jointly determined, as in the European Union, or by the newly formed state, as was the case in the United Kingdom after 1707. For Scotland, the main influences of the Union in the eighteenth and nineteenth centuries were almost certainly manifest through the integration of trade links, with the Empire as well as with England, and through the greater mobility of labour and capital. The economic structure of Victorian Scotland was created within the historical context of imperial and industrial expansion, and the essential and distinctive characteristics of that formative industrial era is thus an essential prerequisite to understanding the more recent past.

Growth and structure

The twentieth century has been a period of massive structural readjustment in Scotland, as it has been in much of the industrialised world. The economic structure which had to adjust to extensive changes in technological advance as well as to intense international competition was established in the substantial expansion achieved in the previous two centuries, but especially in the Victorian years. The economic expansion of the two centuries before the First World War was characterised by increases in population and employment, the growth of the productive process being supported and sustained by increases in labour inputs. In Scotland between 1851 and 1911, population increased from 2.89 million to 4.76 million while employment doubled from one to two million people. In the twentieth century population growth was far more modest reaching five million in mid century while employment remained fairly stable (Figure 1).

The process of structural change involves the creation of new employment and the disappearance of redundant jobs. In the Victorian period the creative effect was far greater than the destructive effect so that there was a massive net increase. But there was some contraction of employment in parts of the economy, principally in agriculture and in textiles and clothing which together had dominated the early Victorian economy accounting for over half the total employment in Scotland in 1851 (Lee 1979: tables). Agricultural employment reached a peak in 1871 and then embarked on a steady decline so that by the eve of the First World War there were 100,000 less workers on the land than there had been 40 years earlier. In the textiles sector, over 60,000 jobs were lost, principally by male workers, between the mid nineteenth century peak and the Great War. In the related clothing trades the peak of employment was reached at the turn of the century after which numbers in this sector declined. But these losses were more than compensated by the substantial increase in employment in other areas of the economy. Furthermore, the Victorian workforce was male dominated, a bias which was increased as the ratio of male to female workers increased from 2/1 to 2.5/1. Between 1841 and 1911 there was a net increase in Scotland of over 760,000 male jobs and 285,000 female jobs. The stimulus given by the First World War further increased male employment by nearly 100,000 by 1921 when it reached its peak level of almost 1,570,000.

Much of this new employment engaged male manual work-

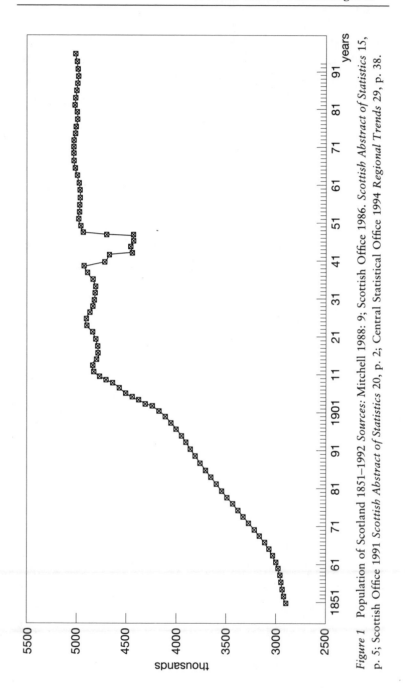

Figure 1 Population of Scotland 1851–1992 *Sources:* Mitchell 1988: 9; Scottish Office 1986. *Scottish Abstract of Statistics* 15, p. 5; Scottish Office 1991 *Scottish Abstract of Statistics* 20, p. 2; Central Statistical Office 1994 *Regional Trends* 29, p. 38.

ers in mining, engineering and metal working, shipbuilding, construction and transport. Male employment in mining increased from 25,000 in 1841 to 165,000 by 1911 and, stimulated by the demands of the First World War, reached a peak of 176,000 in 1921. Shipbuilding employment showed a similar pattern, growing from 4,000 in 1841 to 51,000 in 1911 and 122,000 by 1921. Over the same period there was a net increase in engineering and metal working industries in excess of 200,000 male jobs, and a further 125,000 in the transport sector. Quite clearly the main employment expansion of the Victorian era, reaching its high point with the First World War, was predominantly male and primarily in heavy industry and its ancilliary activities.

It was also heavily concentrated in central Scotland, so that over 60 per cent of the net increase in employment was located in the Strathclyde region and a further 25 per cent in the Lothian region, in Central and Fife. These regions thus acquired highly specialised economic structures. In 1921, the mining, shipbuilding, metal working and engineering industries together accounted for 34.0 per cent of male employment in Scotland. In the Strathclyde and Central and Fife regions this share was 46.1 per cent, while in Lothian it was 28.0 per cent. Elsewhere in Scotland male employment was similarly concentrated. In the Highland region agriculture and fishing accounted for 49.4 per cent of all male employment, as it did for over 30 per cent in Grampian, Dumfries and Galloway and the Borders. In Tayside 17.5 per cent of male employment was in primary production while a further 17.8 per cent was in the textiles and clothing industries. Female employment, as in the rest of the United Kingdom, was concentrated primarily in the service sector and in textiles and clothing at the close of the Victorian era, as indeed it had been at its beginning, increased employment being generated primarily in the former activities. But at the end of the First World War women still comprised only 29 per cent of the Scottish labour force.

The process of production

By the beginning of the twentieth century, Scotland had developed a distinctive industrial structure with even greater reliance on heavy industry than the United Kingdom as a whole. This was indicated in the output structure in the 1907 Census of Production which showed 11.2 per cent of Scottish output derived from mines and quarries compared to 8.4 per cent for the United Kingdom and 30.6 per cent from iron, steel, engineering and shipbuilding compared to 21.3 per cent (Campbell 1980: 197). This industrial concentration, particularly in central Scotland, had a number of defining characteristics which influenced its prospects in the longer term. It was, in the first instance, based on local natural resources of coal, iron ore and water supplies as well as available labour. The iron industry in Scotland was based on local splint coal and indigenous iron ore deposits which had a high phosphorus content. This was not well suited to the malleable iron production required for steel, although this problem could be overcome by using labour intensive methods. Accordingly Scottish iron masters concentrated on pig iron production for sale to foundries which added little to the value of their product. These technical problems discouraged attempts to extend integration into steel manufacture, and persuaded the major iron manufacturers of the virtues of backward integration into coal mining and suitable by-products. The industry remained viable until 1914, declining as resources were exhausted. But production of iron ore reached a peak output in 1880 at a little over 2.6 million tons per year, thereafter falling sharply to under 0.6 million tons in 1913 (Campbell 1980: 101).

The nucleus of the Scottish steel industry was formed in the 1880s by the malleable iron producers. They were frequently independent of pig iron makers, used skilled labour and local coal, and coped with technical problems by adopting labour-intensive methods in small-scale acid open-hearth furnaces. This made possible the use of a certain amount of Scottish iron along with imported ores and scrap. The separation of iron-making from malleable iron manufacture was perpetuated in the separation of iron from steel. In 1900 only three out of fifteen steelworks in Scotland were integrated with blast furnaces (Tolliday 1987: 84–5). By 1914 the weaknesses of Scottish steel production were clearly evident in fragmented small-scale production unable to exploit either economies of scale or the best technology. Scottish steel producers complained about the small scale and poor layout of their plant, but systematically refused to invest in new plant or scrap that in existence. Such structural changes would have required relocation and horizontal integration with closure of some existing plant (Campbell 1980: 124–5). Even before 1914 some steel producers faced difficulties. At the beginning of the century Beardmore was the largest steel making and engineering company in Scotland, but it relied on partnership and finance from Vickers of Barrow-in-Furness in 1902 to fund improvements and reduce the bank overdraft until the rearmament boom averted or rather delayed financial crisis (Hume/Moss 1979: 56, 90).

The coal industry in Scotland had also exploited some of its best reserves before the First World War, although Scottish mines in 1913 were smaller than their counterparts in the rest of Great Britain, employing an average of 301 workers per mine as against the national average of 408. In Scotland 82.9 per cent of miners worked in pits with less than one thousand workers compared to 63.3 per cent nationally (Supple 1987: table 9.2). The Royal Commission on Coal Supplies of 1905 identified Fife as the main area for future development, but expressed reservations about existing fields like Lanarkshire, noting that thinner seams than hitherto were currently being exploited and that some of the cheaper seams were close to being exhausted. By 1914 Lanarkshire had become a high cost coal producer at 57p per ton compared to a cost of about 45p in Ayrshire, Dunbartonshire, West Lothian and Midlothian (Slaven 1975: 169). Furthermore, output per man fell in the western coalfield while productivity in the east increased markedly at the beginning of the century. By then the output share of the western coalfields was declining with Fife and Clackmannan in the ascendent. The industry was already moving away from the proximity of established heavy industry, its principal customer. But 1913 marked the high point of Scottish coal output (Figure 2) and almost all the constituent coalfields experienced an absolute decline in output thereafter (Leser 1954: 113).

By 1914 the heavy industrial complex of the west of Scotland depended on shipbuilding which provided the essential demand for steel, engineering and coal. Indeed the Scottish steel industry was created to supply the requirements of the shipbuilders. The Clydeside yards relied heavily on Admiralty contracts for warships which accounted for about 45 per cent of the total tonnage ordered in the quarter century prior to 1914, and the rearmament boom in the decade before hostilities provided a substantial stimulus (Peebles 1987: 1–2). Prior to 1914 the British industry enjoyed a massive expansion and domination of international markets, retaining 60 per cent of

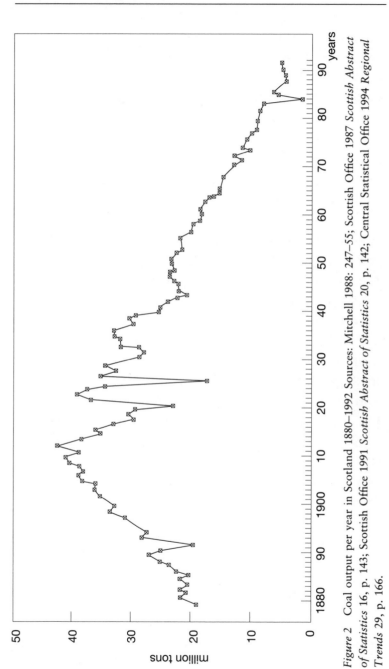

Figure 2 Coal output per year in Scotland 1880–1992 Sources: Mitchell 1988: 247–55; Scottish Office 1987 *Scottish Abstract of Statistics* 16, p. 143; Scottish Office 1991 *Scottish Abstract of Statistics* 20, p. 142; Central Statistical Office 1994 *Regional Trends* 29, p. 166.

world sales at the turn of the century. About one third of the tonnage launched from British yards between 1870 and 1913 was built on the Clyde, and in the final year of peace the Clyde yards launched 18 per cent of world tonnage.

In terms of capital value, Victorian business operated on a massive scale only in the form of railway companies and financial institutions. By market value the largest 100 companies in 1904–05 included relatively few manufacturers. More than two thirds of the capital invested in the 60 largest Scottish firms was in railway stock, and over half of that was invested in two massive companies, the Caledonian Railway and the North British Railway. The £121 million invested in the railways dwarfed that in iron, steel and engineering, together worth £13.5 million, in textiles a further £13.4 million and in food and drink, some £6.6 million (Scott and Hughes 1980: 19). The two major Scottish railways appear high in the individual company ranking within the United Kingdom. The Caledonian Railway (6th) had a market value of £58.2 million and the North British Railway (7th) a market value of £58.0 million. The only Scottish manufacturer, and the largest manufacturer in the entire list, was the Paisley thread producer J & P Coats (12th) with a market value of £42.1 million (Wardley 1991: 278). By comparison the heavy industries were smaller operations. The North British Locomotive Company, formed in 1903 from the amalgamation of three Glasgow companies and, at that time, the major British locomotive manufacturer, had a capital of £2 million (Campbell 1978: 201). Amongst the shipbuilding firms, John Brown and Company had a capital value of £3.4 million in 1912, while Beardmore was valued at £2 million. They were the largest in Scotland and within the industry were smaller only than Vickers and Armstrong Whitworth (Pollard and Robertson 1979: 81). The rest of the Clydeside yards were valued at less than £1 million. But some of these manufacturers do appear on the list of major employers. John Brown and Company had a workforce of 20,000 in six different locations in 1907, the Fife Coal Company 13,000, J & P Coats 12,700, Stewarts and Lloyds (steel) 10,600, the North British Locomotive Company 7,850, Fairfield Shipbuilding and Engineering 6,000, the Steel Company of Scotland 6,000, the Wemyss Coal Company and Beardmore both 4,500, although they were smaller than the major railway companies with over 20,000 employees each (Jeremy 1991: 96–9).

These relative concentrations of capital and labour reflect the labour intensity of Victorian industry. In 1890, it has been estimated, labour costs amounted to half the total cost of finished steel in Scotland and between 33 and 66 per cent in shipbuilding. Data from John Brown and Company for 1890–95 indicated that labour costs made up between 31 and 49 per cent of the cost of the hull of a sample of 30 vessels (Campbell 1980: 16–17). As late as 1910 the total value of machinery in Brown's Clydebank yard was only £200,000 with very small sums per worker (Pollard and Robertson 1979: 127). Cheap iron and steel, and labour, were important inputs in shipbuilding. Few new yards contributed to this expansion. Production was increased by the purchase of derelict or bankrupt yards, or by the extension of existing facilities. The firms remained relatively small, a necessity if the need for external capital was to be avoided. On the eve of the First World War over one quarter of the major shipbuilding firms had a board of directors confined to members of the same family. The £7 million capital vested in the limited shipyards on the Clyde was primarily held in shares which were privately owned and not quoted on the financial markets. Some had limited liability thrust upon them by circumstance, death duties in the case of William Denny and Brothers, the death of a major partner in the case of Alexander Stephen and Sons (Pollard and Robertson 1979: 76). This industry was renowned for its small scale of production in independent shipyards relying heavily on craft manual skills. A survey taken in 1911 found that 67 per cent of Scottish shipyard workers were skilled men. There was little standardised production, indeed specialisation had been encouraged by the scale and range of demand in the Victorian decades. Some mechanisation primarily assisted existing craft work, and did not supplant or deskill the labour force. But it has been argued that labour conflicts from the 1880s onwards reflected the resistance of skilled workers to replacement by semi-automatic machinery and unskilled labour, and that after the turn of the century mechanisation allowed the substitution of skilled by unskilled workers (Lorenz and Wilkinson 1986: 111–12; Knox *et al.* 1993: 200–9). The combination of skilled labour and extensive specialisation of function enabled the shipyards to operate with low fixed costs, and thence limited capital investment. But output per worker remained substantially higher than that achieved in German or American yards at the time (Pagnamenta and Overy 1984: 126).

Prior to the First World War most of the ownership and control of Scottish industry lay within Scotland, since many businesses were owned and controlled by those who operated them, as part of the long tradition of family firms. To that extent Scotland was economically separate. Some companies did move to Scotland from bases elsewhere, Yarrow's shipyard was originally located on the Thames before moving to the Clyde, while John Brown's started as a Sheffield steel manufacturer. But many major firms were indigenous to Scotland and some extended their activities and reputations worldwide like Jardine Matheson and J & P Coats. A series of interlocking directorships, based in Glasgow around the interests of the Caledonian Railway, held the heavy industries together in a network which included Lanarkshire coal, iron and railway interests, the Highland Railway, and the Tennant empire which included Tharsis Sulphur and Copper, the Steel Company of Scotland, Nobel's Explosives and Young's Paraffin Oil. But there were equally impressive networks in the east, based around the vitally important but often overlooked element in the Scottish economy, the financial sector. Banks, insurance companies, investment and property companies, mainly based in Edinburgh, some of which were impressively large institutions, created a pattern of linkages in the east which brought together the North British Railway with the Royal Bank, the Linen Bank and numerous investment companies (Scott and Hughes 1980: 41–2).

Some growth was achieved through mergers and amalgamations. John Brown and Company added shipbuilding to steel manufacturing by purchasing J & G Thomson's shipyard at Clydebank in 1899. Both Vickers and Armstrong Whitworth secured shares in Beardmore in the 1900s, while many individuals held directorships which extended across a range of steel making, engineering, ordnance and shipbuilding activities. In 1913 Barclay Curle and Company of Glasgow merged with the Tyneside yard of Swan Hunter and Wigham Richardson, an expansion which generated a sufficient scale of production to secure Admiralty orders for warships. Cammel Laird of Birkenhead secured shares in Fairfield Shipbuilding of Govan before 1914 while Fairfield and John Brown held shares in the Coventry Ordnance Works. But the flow of funds and ownership was not simply from south to north. Major Scottish companies extended their interests further afield. Standard

Life Assurance of Edinburgh, one of the dominant companies within United Kingdom financial circles, had acquired a diverse portfolio of investments by 1913, including an interest in the Barrow Shipbuilding Company, Denaby and Cadeby Main Colliery, the Irwell Bank Spinning Company and about £1.6 million in land mortgages and municipal securities in Canada (Treble 1980: 183).

Incomes and consumer demand

The rise and fall of great industries, which catches the attention and fires the imagination of many historians, is only a part of the economic process. Equally significant is the contribution of that economic activity to the welfare of society. The aim of economic advance is, after all, to augment the living standards of as many of the population and to as great a degree as possible. Further, consumer spending has become a critical element in economic advance, as high wages and resultant spending not only provide gratification for the individual concerned but create demand for the goods and services which, in turn, provides the employment and incomes for others. The distribution of the fruits of Victorian industrialisation was thus of great importance. It was also extremely inequitable for the great fortunes acquired by some captains of industry stand against the enduring poverty of many in Victorian Scotland.

Rubinstein's compilation of the largest fortunes in Britain, those of £2 million or more, left between 1809 and 1914 contained five in Scotland out of a total of forty. All were Clydeside industrialists; William Baird the ironmaster, Sir Charles Tennant head of the chemical empire, Peter Coats and Sir James Coats the thread manufacturers, and William Weir an ironmaster and colliery owner who was also a nephew of Baird (Rubinstein 1987: 30–2). There were also landowners with Scottish estates, such as the Duke of Sutherland and the Marquis of Bute. All the estimates of wealth and taxable income indicated the overwhelming dominance of the metropolitan economy with the manufacturing centres some way behind, even though probate inventories understate the value of landed property. Scotland, doubtless due to the industrialisation of Clydeside, appears in most rankings close to industrial regions like Yorkshire and Lancashire. The distribution of taxpayers in 1900–01, when Scotland had 12.1 per cent of the population of Great Britain, gave Scotland's share at 4.6 per cent for incomes over £10,000, at 7.6 per cent for incomes between £1,000 and £10,000, and 10.2 per cent for taxable incomes under £1,000 (Rubinstein 1987: 113). Outside London and the main English industrial counties, Scotland fared reasonably well in terms of these middle class incomes.

But a less optimistic interpretation is suggested by a study of wage rates. Since labour, even skilled labour, was relatively abundant its reward in terms of wages was modest. Scottish wages were generally lower than those in England although the gap narrowed in the course of the nineteenth century. But they were still at least 5 per cent lower according to the most optimistic reading of the 1886 census. Compared to the United Kingdom average Scottish wages were low in most textiles trades (£28 per annum in cotton as against £36), in iron and steel, and shipbuilding (£70 against £76) and brewing (£52 against £60). By the time of the 1906 Wages Census, Scotland compared favourably with the United Kingdom average in most trades (Campbell 1980: 191–4). On the basis of the rather heroic assumption that workers enjoyed 50 weeks employment per annum, a full time male worker in iron and steel manu-

facture would have obtained £102.50 per year, a Clyde shipyard worker and a tailor £90, a printer £87.50, and an engineer or boilermaker £82.50. These were the best returns.
Women and juveniles were paid substantially less, often under
50 per cent of the adult male rate, and men employed in public
utilities received under £75 per annum in most occupations.
These incomes should be placed in the perspective of white
collar workers. Estimates for annual earnings in the United
Kingdom in 1913/14 included solicitors £568, barristers £478,
general practitioners £395, dentists £368, engineers £292, cler-
gymen £206 and male school teachers £154 (Routh 1980: 60,
73). The annual income for a coalface miner in 1906 was estimated at £112, and for a railway engine driver £119. These
were the cream of the skilled manual trades, manufacturing
work averaged £90 per annum (Routh 1980: 98–100). The real
importance of wage rates depends, therefore, less on the relative differences between regions but on the composition of
employment within each economy.

   In the context of Edwardian Britain the assumption of full
employment is hardly warranted. Estimates of average earnings rather than full employment earnings in the 1906 Wages
Census reduce, for example, iron and steel earnings from
£102.50 to £92.50 per annum, and shipyard earnings from £90
to £82.50. Estimates of unemployment in engineering and shipbuilding between 1902–14 placed Scotland above the national
average. In engineering the unemployment rate was 9.20 per
cent in the east of Scotland and 7.72 per cent in Glasgow and
district, as compared to a national average of 5.38 per cent.
The unemployment rate for east coast shipyards averaged
15.55 per cent and for the Clyde at 10.53 per cent a better than
average performance, the national rate being 11.04 per cent
(Southall 1988: 246–7). But these figures are high enough to

make substantial inroads into the incomes of a primarily skilled craft group. Nor indeed was unemployment the only threat to income. Underemployment was common in activities where piece rates prevailed. The earnings of riveters on the Clyde in the 1900s suggested an average of £75 per annum but with a substantial variation about that average. Gangs which secured only low pay were often characterised by part-time working, through absenteeism, injury or lack of opportunity, while the introduction of hydraulic riveting machinery removed some of the most rewarding jobs, leaving the residual tasks to apprentices who were, in effect, mobile and cheap workers (Price 1981: 59). Much lower paid work was also casual and the proportion of such workers in the labour force has been estimated at between 20–27 per cent of total employment in the four major Scottish cities (Treble 1979: 115–42). Employment could also be erratic. In Denny's shipyard at Leven the workforce ranged from 1,116 to 2,622 between 1885 and 1913. Furthermore, living costs appear to have been relatively high. A survey taken in 1905 of the cost of buying a bundle of essential commodities put Scotland a little above the London price level and ten per cent above major cities in the north and midlands. In 1912 the Board of Trade estimated that real wages in Scottish towns were 10 per cent less than in their English counterparts (Rodger 1989: 32).

One of the manifestations of poor wages is a low level of consumer demand, and one of the ways in which this appears is in a low multiplier effect in creating additional work in the service industries. In 1911 most regions of Scotland were relatively poorly provided with service sector employment with serious implications for spending power not least because some service sector employment, as in the professions, was relatively well paid. Scotland had 1.3 jobs per thousand popu-

lation less than the national average in 1911 (Lee 1983: 32).
Raising that provision to the average would have added over
6,000 professional workers to the Scottish labour force.
Assuming a modest average salary of £200 per annum, this
would have added some £1.2 million to spending power. The
difference in service employment provision between Scotland
and Great Britain as a whole was greatest in the miscellaneous
services category which, at this time, contained a large number
of domestic servants. These jobs were not well paid, but the
deficiency in employment, of close to 100,000 in Scotland,
reflects not just lost work opportunities but limited middle
class demand for these were the social groups who sustained
domestic service in the late nineteenth century. Overall had
Scottish service sector employment ratios been raised to
national levels in 1911 the labour force would have been
increased by 6.7 per cent. The weak multiplier effect denoted
by service sector provision was greatest in the heart of the
industrial regions, in Strathclyde and in Central and Fife. In
these regions provision at the national level would have
increased employment by 8.4 per cent and 14.8 per cent respectively.

Scottish housing

One of the most distinctive features of the Scottish economy
in the past century has been the poor state of housing inherited from the Victorian era, itself a most potent indicator of
the limitations of Victorian industrialisation as a means of creating general prosperity. The dreadful state of housing in Scotland was expounded by the Royal Commission which reported
in 1917;

These are the broad results of our survey: unsatisfactory sites

of houses and villages, insufficient supplies of water, unsatisfactory provision for drainage, grossly inadequate provision for
the removal of refuse, widespread absence of decent sanitary
conveniences, the persistence of the unspeakably filthy privy-
midden in many of the mining areas, badly constructed, incur-
ably damp labourers' cottages on farms, whole townships unfit
for human occupation in the crofting counties and islands,
primitive and casual provision for many of the seasonal workers, gross over-crowding and huddling of the sexes together in
the congested industrial villages and towns, occupation of one-
room houses by large families, groups of lightless and unventi-
lated houses in the older burghs, clotted masses of slums in the
great cities. To these add the special problems symbolised by
farmed-out houses, and model lodging houses, congested back-
lands and ancient closes. To these, again, add the cottages a
hundred years old in some of the rural villages, ramshackle
brick survivals of the mining outbursts of seventy years ago in
the mining fields, monotonous miners' rows flung down without a vestige of town plan or any effort to secure modern conditions of sanitation, ill-planned houses that must become
slums in a few years, old houses converted without the necessary sanitary appliances and proper adaptation into tenements
for many families, thus intensifying existing evils, streets of new
tenements in the towns developed with the minimum regard for
amenity (Royal Commission on the Housing ... of Scotland
1917: 346).

The limitations on consumer demand imposed by modest and
variable incomes were manifest in the demand for housing.
Small houses were characteristic of Scotland. In 1911 while
73.8 per cent of houses in England and Wales had four rooms
or more, in Scotland the proportion was 26.5 per cent. The
main improvement which occurred in Scotland in the half century before 1914 was that the proportion of families living in
a single room fell from 34 to 20 per cent of the total while
those living in two or three rooms rose from 52 to 65 per cent

(Butt 1971: 81). The construction of houses with three apartments or less constituted 85 per cent of the addition to the total stock in the second half of the century and many houses were created by subdividing existing properties. The quality of housing was poor. The tenement was the distinctive form of Scottish home compared to the two storey cottage which was so prevalent in English towns and which afforded more privacy than the communal washing, drying and toilet facilities of the tenements. Such homes were not confined to the poorer sections of society. The development of the West End of Glasgow in the late nineteenth century included tenement flats designed for middle class professional workers owned by doctors, engineers, teachers and merchants and tenanted by members of those occupations as well as dentists, accountants and shopkeepers (Atherton 1991: 25).

At the lower end of the housing market in Edinburgh and Glasgow in 1915, over 90 per cent of single roomed houses and a substantial proportion of two roomed properties shared a water closet (Rodger 1986: 162). Overcrowding was a common problem. By the standard measurement of overcrowding as more than two persons per room, over 60 per cent of the population of Airdrie, Motherwell, Barrhead, Clydebank and Port Glasgow were so disadvantaged, a rate ten times that prevailing in major English cities. The most favoured major Scottish city, Edinburgh, which had about one third of its population living in overcrowded conditions, was similar to the worst areas in England such as Tyneside or the East End of London (Rodger 1989: 27). While the proportion of those living in overcrowded conditions in the Scottish cities fell in the second half of the nineteenth century, population growth meant that their numbers actually grew. But the incidence of poverty meant that periodically a substantial number of houses remained untenanted. On the eve of the First World War, over 20,000 houses remained unoccupied in Glasgow alone, about one tenth of the entire housing stock of the city (Butt 1971: 63).

Overcrowded housing conditions were linked with other manifestations of poverty. Variations in infant mortality, a prime indicator of relative deprivation, were greatest between regions of Britain just after the First World War. Statistical estimation suggested that high rates of infant mortality, as in Scotland, were associated with high density living accommodation and were especially prevalent in mining communities (Lee 1991: 63). Another series of estimates based on data for 1911 for districts of Glasgow found that infant mortality rates were directly linked to the number of persons per room in households, the prevalence of one-roomed houses and, inversely, to large houses with four or five rooms (Cage 1994: 87).

The weakness of effective demand was compounded by important supply side constraints on Scottish house building. Land tenure in Scotland differed from that south of the border in that a vendor relinquished the title to land but retained the right to an annual payment of feu-duty. This encouraged landowners to hold their property until prices were high so that they would receive a large feu-duty payment in perpetuity since it could not be adjusted once set. Furthermore, entitlement to feu-duty passed successively with the transfer of land, creating a chain of obligations whereby each individual had to pay his immediate superior in the chain. In order to cover for defaulters the duty was set at a high level for everyone. Since feu-duty was the first claim on any bankrupt estate it provided a secure basis for raising capital, so much so that builders offered the right to farm inflated feu-duties in return for capital advances for building. All these factors conspired to raise the price of land and thus building costs. Land charges added 10–14 per cent to the gross rental of tenement properties, and reinforced the pressure towards the construction of high rise buildings (Rodger 1989: 33). Scottish building regulations added further costs. For a three-storey dwelling, wall thickness regulations in London were substantially less stringent than those operating in Glasgow, which 'resulted in a 25 per cent increase in the quantity of materials; in addition, to support the heavier weight of the walls, and the stiffer code regarding roof materials, depths of foundations had to be increased, adding 73 per cent to the equivalent London costs. In a one-storey building the requirements of the Glasgow byelaws for walls and foundations imposed on average a 40 per cent excess on the London specifications' (Rodger 1986: 185). The London specifications were widely adopted throughout England while the Glasgow regulations were regarded by many in the construction industry as being unnecessarily severe, and thus wasteful as well as an impediment to building. But by 1900 over 200 Scottish burghs enforced minimum building regulations which covered sanitation and safety standards, and this fed through into higher rents.

The supply of housing was also influenced by the instability of the construction industry rooted in the prevalence of small firms operating on a hand to mouth basis. These builders found their costs increasing steadily in the late nineteenth century, by 40 per cent between 1880 and 1914, fuelled by rising labour costs and the stringent building regulations. The erosion of profits and upward movements in expectations regarding standards of accommodation rendered working class house building increasingly unprofitable. Builders and landlords accordingly reduced their involvement in this lowest sector of the housing market. The weakness in the housing market was demonstrated by the sharp downturn in construction in Scotland in the decade before the First World War.

Attempts to involve local authorities in housing provision which was permitted by the legislation of 1890, was circumscribed by the ratepayers. The growth of municipal responsibilities in the late nineteenth century, partly imposed by central government and partly assumed by local councils, imposed a growing strain on finances which were derived from taxation on property. This obviously imposed greater burdens on the better quality and larger properties, and the effective subsidy this entailed generated conflicts between the parties involved. Local authorities sought to raise more revenue from a limited tax base while house proprietors opposed rate increases. Scottish landlords were additionally disadvantaged, compared to their English counterparts in that undeveloped land was largely exempt from rates which, in Scotland, were calculated on gross rather than net rentals. On the other hand it was to the advantage of the owner that in Scotland, until 1957, rates were paid jointly by tenant and owner. The rates were determined by the size of the rent, so that an owner could increase the rent and offset in full his or her share of additional rates while thereby increasing the value of the property.

The influences of both supply costs and deficient demand were brought together in the leasing arrangements which in Scotland were characterised by annual contracts, compared to the weekly tenure common in England and Wales.

The practice of yearly letting had serious disadvantages for the Scot. First, and most conspicuously, in the context of unusually variable employment prospects the standard of accommodation affordable over one year's lease had to take account of interrupted earnings. English short lets allowed a tenant, in extremis, to move to cheaper accommodation or to move easily

to another location for employment purposes, though it has
been argued that in fact this was more urgently required in
Scottish towns (Rodger 1986: 189).

One other result was that eviction rates were far higher in
Scotland than in the south. An eviction warrant in London in
1886–90 was served for every 1,818 inhabitants compared to
the Glasgow rate of one for every 54. Furthermore, Scottish
rents were high compared to those elsewhere in Britain other
than London. A survey taken in 1905 placed, Edinburgh and
Leith, Glasgow, Dundee, Greenock, Paisley, Falkirk, Aberdeen
and Kilmarnock in descending order in the top 15 local
authorities (Rodger 1986: 195). Working class rents in Scotland were thus about 10 per cent higher than in Northumberland and Durham and up to 25 per cent higher than in other
areas in the north and midlands of England.

By the eve of the First World War, Scotland stood on the
brink of a housing catastrophe. The increasing gap between
rents obtainable in a weak market and the construction costs
of properties built by the private sector reduced supply and
gave rise to a powerful lobby for the reducing of building
standards and sanitary requirements by the turn of the century. At the same time, by the definition of overcrowding being
more than two persons per room, over two million Scots,
nearly half the population, were so housed. In 1917 the Royal
Commission estimated an immediate need for 236,000 new
houses without regard to the lack of construction in the war
which probably would have increased the total to over
300,000, a massive addition to the existing stock (Begg 1987:
7–8).

Flawed development: a legacy of union?

The economic structure established in nineteenth-century Scotland provided the framework for the adjustments of the present century. It is an era about which there has developed a substantial mythology, extolling the glories of Victorian industrialisation, encouraged as much by myopic historians as by politicians looking for some past golden age. The economic achievements of the Victorians were certainly substantial. It was a remarkable feat to launch one sixth of the world's shipping from Clydeside berths in 1913. Considerable wealth and employment were created. But there were crucial limitations to the process which became apparent after the First World War. The heavy industry of central Scotland was founded on a very limited resource base. By 1913 the iron ore reserves were rapidly approaching exhaustion while coal production reached its peak in that year. The weakness of the iron ore resource and its unsuitability for steel created an almost unprecedented division between iron and steel manufacture. Furthermore, all these industries relied, in the last resort, on the prosperity of shipbuilding for the demand for their products. In their turn, the shipyards relied on exports. The entire industrial structure was thus dependent on competitive success in a relatively narrow range of activity.

There are other indicators which show the partiality of this growth. In the late nineteenth century there was a massive outflow of investment from Scotland, as indeed there was from the rest of the United Kingdom, increasing from £60 million in 1870 to £500 million by 1914. At this latter date, overseas investment stood at £90 per head of population for the United Kingdom as a whole, but in Scotland it was even higher at £110 per head (Harvie 1994: 70). This reflected opportunities overseas, but confirmed the limited demand in the domestic economy which was most obviously revealed in poor living standards, enduring poverty and the almost uniquely poor state of housing in Scotland. The gains from Victorian industrialisation were thus shared with extreme inequality between members of that society, they rested on a highly vulnerable resource base, and they did not significantly contribute towards the establishment of a consumer-led economy or markedly ameliorate the widespread poverty.

Would an independent Scotland have fared better? To answer that requires an assessment of what might have been the most likely economic development path for a Scottish economy which remained independent in the two centuries after 1707. Exclusion from the English and Empire markets in the eighteenth century would certainly have constituted a considerable disadvantage, particularly as the trade barriers of that time were specifically intended to protect the domestic agricultural sector and industries such as textiles. The cattle and linen trades would have been severely restricted as the British tariff protected land-intensive production until the 1840s. The duty on imports fell quickly in the nineteenth century from a peak in the 1820s when it reached over 50 per cent of the value of imports to less than 10 per cent of that value by the 1870s (Harley 1994: 314). So the establishment of free trade in the Victorian boom would have allowed Scotland access to English and imperial markets as well as to the rest of the world. There seems little doubt that Scottish industry in the nineteenth century did follow an optimising development path by exploiting natural resources of iron, coal and shipbuilding facilities, as well as through the export of capital. From this perspective it seems likely that exclusion from the Union would have been detrimental in the later eighteenth century but that the effect would have become neutral by the Victorian period. In this later phase of economic growth the Union was primarily permissive, providing access to the market opportunities of the Empire and international economy. The free mobility of labour and capital provided Scots with both career and investment opportunities which were available outside as well as within the Union. Much of the outward migration from Scotland headed for the United States, so that exclusion from the Union seems unlikely to have adversely affected labour mobility, while the massive export of capital from Victorian Scotland does not suggest that there were serious financial constraints on growth.

The case for a neutral verdict on the impact of the Union on the Victorian economy is strengthened by two other considerations. In the context of free trade, government policy was essentially permissive and the state did not intrude on economic and social matters very extensively. Furthermore, the control of all sectors of business and thus the entire Scottish economy still remained principally in the hands of Scots. The economic and social order of Victorian Scotland was homemade. As one authority observed, 'The ruling elites in this regional economy were so successful both in business and in the creation and manipulation of political and social controls over the poorly-paid bulk of the population that they preserved the hierarchic order which suited them with remarkable continuity between 1840 and 1914' (Lenman 1977: 204).

Prior to the twentieth century, therefore, it seems very probable that the Union offered opportunities without serious constraints. The looseness of both political and economic control exerted by central government allowed all the regional economies within the United Kingdom to follow their own distinctive patterns of economic development within the permis-

sive framework of a vast imperial network of market opportunities. It is difficult to make any serious case for the Union
acting as an obstacle to Scottish economic advance in the two
hundred years following its inception except possibly during
the very short-term adjustment process in the years immediately after 1707. On the other hand, it is difficult to identify
any obvious development path for the Scottish economy
during these centuries other than through specialised production for the export trade. In both the eighteenth and nineteenth
centuries access to the markets of England and its imperial territories offered far better opportunities than anywhere else,
not least because much of Europe was protected by tariff barriers. This clear balance of economic opportunity may partly
explain why discontent with the Union in Scotland remained
confined to the political periphery until the present century.

Chapter 3

The patterns of structural change

Growth, convergence and divergence

Throughout the world economy, the twentieth century has been a period of both unprecedented economic growth and structural change, the latter being manifest most obviously in changing levels and forms of production and employment. Economic vulnerability has been manifest, and most widely perceived, in unemployment growth as the negative aspect of structural change. In the industrial world, the interwar period and the past two decades have been characterised by relatively high and enduring levels of unemployment. This has reflected both the transient phases of the economic cycle and an underlying structural change away from some pursuits with a long historical tradition, like agriculture and mining, to activities more obviously characteristic of a higher income society, like financial and professional services, and this has been augmented by shifts in productivity which have differentially adjusted the demand for labour between sectors of the economy. The scale of structural change, in employment and production, has been greater in the twentieth century than hitherto, and has engendered political and economic conflict thoughout the industrial economies of the western world. All these influences have been manifest in Scotland, and the critical reassessment which such problems have stimulated has focused attention on the balance of benefits or penalties which have accrued from membership of the Union.

For much of the twentieth century the growth of the gross domestic product (GDP) of the United Kingdom has been close to its long-term annual rate of 2 per cent. It averaged 2.2 per cent between 1924 and 1937, a rather better 2.8 per cent between 1951 and 1973, and 2.3 per cent, erratically, through the 1980s. During the two wartime periods, performance was much weaker, as it was in the 1973–79 period when it averaged 1.3 per cent (Lee 1986: 5). For subdivisions of the United Kingdom, like Scotland, estimates are rather less certain. Campbell's figures for the interwar period suggested a much poorer Scottish performance, averaging 0.4 per cent per annum with an absolute decline of 20 per cent in the depression from 1928 to 1932 (Campbell 1954: 50). Thereafter wartime revival and inflationary pressure produced an annual growth rate of 8 per cent over the decade 1938–48, far higher than in the United Kingdom as a whole. Throughout the postwar period, Scotland has enjoyed a growth rate of GDP rather less than that of the United Kingdom although this has been marked by buoyant phases, as from 1963 to 1976 and in the past few years, with some comparatively weak phases, as in the 1950s, the later 1970s and the mid 1980s. In per capita terms, Scotland has remained below the United Kingdom average, moving sharply upward towards that average between 1934 and 1944, 1963 and 1976 and 1989 and 1991, falling badly behind in the 1920s, 1950s and 1980s (Figure 3).

It should not be assumed that this performance indicates a uniquely poor showing relative to all the remaining areas of the United Kingdom. Such is not the case. The United King-

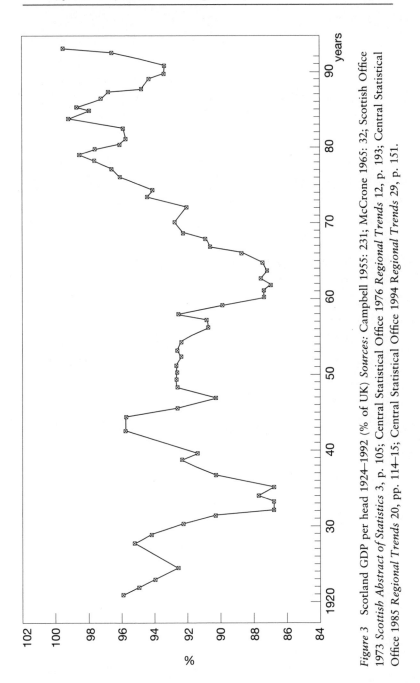

Figure 3 Scotland GDP per head 1924–1992 (% of UK) *Sources:* Campbell 1955: 231; McCrone 1965: 32; Scottish Office 1973 *Scottish Abstract of Statistics* 3, p. 105; Central Statistical Office 1976 *Regional Trends* 12, p. 193; Central Statistical Office 1985 *Regional Trends* 20, pp. 114–15; Central Statistical Office 1994 *Regional Trends* 29, p. 151.

dom economy is heavily influenced by the very large and
extremely prosperous economy of the South East of England
which, in 1992, accounted for 30.5 of total population and 35.4
per cent of national income. So great is the affluence of this
region relative to the rest of the United Kingdom that few
other regions ever achieve an income per head above the
national average. In 1991 the South East stood 17.3 per cent
above the United Kingdom figure for GDP per head. Only one
other region, East Anglia, was above the national average,
marginally so by 0.4 per cent, followed by the East Midlands
at 97.1 per cent and Scotland at 95.8 per cent of that aggregate
figure (*Regional Trends* 29:151, 176–7). All the other regions
fell in the range 5–20 per cent below the national average,
Wales at 85.1 per cent and Northern Ireland at 81.1 per cent
faring worst.

Over the past thirty years this pattern has remained fairly
stable, and Scotland's position in the regional income ranking
has been similar to that of industrial areas such as Yorkshire
and Humberside, the North West and, latterly since the
decline of the motor industry, the West Midlands, although
Scotland has done rather better in the most recent recession.
In the longer term of the entire twentieth century, Scotland has
occupied a position in the middle range of the United Kingdom per capita income distribution. In relation to the extremes
of the national income distribution, represented by the South
East at one tail and the North and Wales at the other, Scotland has occupied a central position which has remained stable
recently with little sign of convergence from either direction
(Figure 4). In contrast there has been evident convergence
between Scotland and those industrial regions of the United
Kingdom which are most similar in size and structure. In this
latter context, Scotland has fared relatively well in recent

decades (Figure 5). This rather confused pattern of partial convergence and partial stability in differentials is further complicated by recent estimates for regional income within Scotland (Table 1). This demonstrates that there was both an extremely wide variation within Scotland in the 1980s and that there was a marked increase in divergence. At one extreme Grampian stood far above the United Kingdom or Scottish average, exceeded in 1991 only by Central London, while Lothian region came in the top seven areas, defined as the English counties and Scottish and Welsh regions (*Regional Trends* 29: 176–7). On the other hand, all the remaining regions of Scotland fell more than 10 per cent below the national average, although none recorded the very poorest relative performances which identified blackspots such as County Durham, Northumberland, Cornwall, Merseyside, Mid Glamorgan, Dyfed and Gwynedd. Even so, the Highlands and Islands region was identified as being eligible for Objective One status in the European Community, from January 1994, as a 'lagging region', a distinction shared within the United Kingdom with Northern Ireland and Merseyside (*Regional Trends* 29: 164).

Table 1 Regional GDP per head in Scotland (UK=100)

	1981	1984	1987	1989	1991
Strathclyde	89.8	89.7	89.6	88.8	88.3
Dumfries/Galloway	94.3	94.1	88.6	86.8	86.6
Borders	87.2	87.4	92.4	84.2	81.5
Lothian	102.7	105.9	103.9	102.1	110.5
Central	100.9	87.9	93.7	94.4	87.7
Fife	98.7	94.3	84.1	80.8	84.7
Tayside	89.7	91.4	87.9	86.4	89.1
Grampian	120.5	130.3	117.5	120.5	134.8
Highland	99.2	83.1	84.5	78.8	87.3
Scotland	96.3	96.1	93.9	92.7	95.8

Sources: Scottish Office. 1990. *Scottish Economic Bulletin*, 42. Table 4.6; Scottish Office. 1992. *Scottish Economic Bulletin*, 45. Table 4.6; Central Statistical Office. 1994. *Regional Trends*, 29, p. 177.

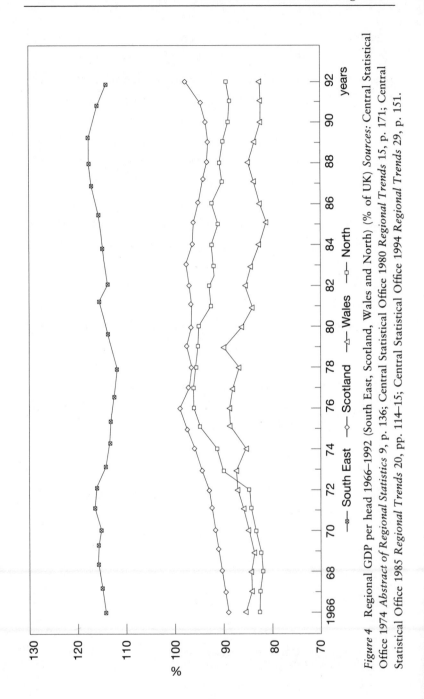

Figure 4 Regional GDP per head 1966–1992 (South East, Scotland, Wales and North) (% of UK) *Sources:* Central Statistical Office 1974 *Abstract of Regional Statistics* 9, p. 136; Central Statistical Office 1980 *Regional Trends* 15, p. 171; Central Statistical Office 1985 *Regional Trends* 20, pp. 114–15; Central Statistical Office 1994 *Regional Trends* 29, p. 151.

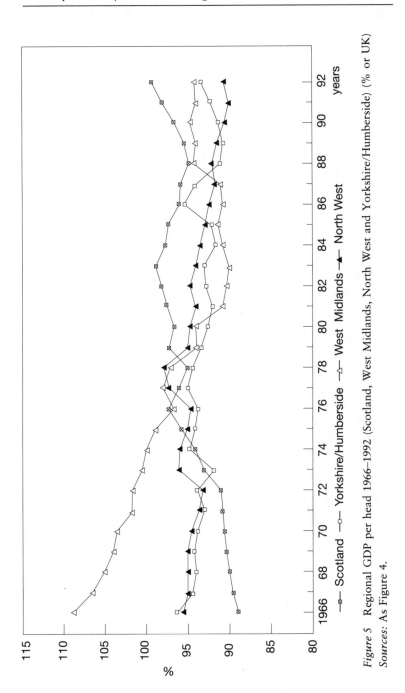

Figure 5 Regional GDP per head 1966–1992 (Scotland, West Midlands, North West and Yorkshire/Humberside) (% or UK)
Sources: As Figure 4.

Production

In terms of production the Census of Production data for gross output indicate, for Scotland, an annual rate of growth of 3.79 per cent between 1907 and 1924, a contraction of 2.89 per cent between 1924 and 1935 and a resumed increase at 6.44 per cent between 1935 and 1948 (Campbell 1980: 197, 202; Leser 1954: 73). Both the interwar contraction and wartime expansion was primarily determined by output changes in mines and quarries, and in iron and steel, engineering and shipbuilding whose combined share of output fell from 41.4 per cent of the total in 1907 to 31.1 per cent in 1935 before reviving to 43.0 per cent in 1948. Buxton's estimates of industrial concentration based on 1929 data showed Scotland heavily committed to jute, marine engineering, carpets, shipbuilding and repairing, constructional engineering, hosiery, linen, pig iron manufacture food, drink and tobacco, and general engineering. Not surprisingly, in 1935, Scotland depended on the 'old' staple industries of the Victorian era for 36.8 per cent of output compared to the 27.8 per cent for the United Kingdom, although the value of the output of mines and quarries fell by £12 million between 1924 and 1935 while that of iron, steel, engineering and shipbuilding fell by over £20 million (Buxton 1980: 548–9; Campbell 1980: 197, 201–2).

It was apparent at the time that Scotland was rather poorly represented in the newer branches of manufacture, such as electrical engineering, motor and cycle manufacture, chemicals, and consumer goods like furniture and upholstery. Buxton's study showed that in 1935 Scotland derived only 11.0 per cent of output from the 'new' industries while the comparable share for the United Kingdom was 21.0 per cent. Similarly, the measure of relative concentration of industry in 1929 showed Scotland to be relatively deficient in textiles and clothing, electrical engineering, chemicals, metal trades, and the construction and repair of motor vehicles. Like many others, Buxton concluded that the failure to develop new specialisms as a balance to the declining heavy industries was a major contributor to the problems of the Scottish economy between the wars as well as consolidating the reliance on heavy industry. Indeed many of the new industries had existed in Scotland before 1914 but had failed to thrive in the 1920s, such as motor vehicle manufacture. These deficiencies had important multiplier effects. Electrical engineering in Scotland was tied into the shipbuilding industry, but Scotland produced very little in terms of electrical generators, motors, power transformers, valves, batteries, radio or telephone equipment. Nor did it have the chemical industry which formed the base for the expanding plastics and paint industries. Even where such industries were represented in the Scottish economy, as many were, their low rate of growth between the wars constituted a relative decline as against the rest of the country, the effect of an unfavourable structure was thus compounded by poor performance (Leser and Silvey 1950: 174). Ministry of Labour data on 23 growth industries between 1923–37 showed that central Scotland had both a modest share at the beginning of that period and a small share of the employment subsequently generated (Saville 1985: 11).

Sectoral data for Scottish gross domestic product are available only from the 1950s. Estimates of structure for that decade suggest only modest differences between the composition of Scottish output and that of the United Kingdom, Scotland being rather more oriented towards agriculture, forestry and fishing, and public services while being relatively light in distribution, financial services and, rather surprisingly, manufacturing. When the composition of manufacturing is compared with that for the United Kingdom in the 1950s the main difference appeared to be Scotland's relative deficiency in vehicle manufacture, chemicals and metal goods, and a relative concentration on food, drink and tobacco, metal manufacture and shipbuilding with marine engineering (McCrone 1965: 33, 54). This structure of production had been sustained with minor modifications throughout the first half of the century.

Several clear trends emerge from a sectoral disaggregation of the sources of postwar Scottish growth (Table 2). Both manufacturing and services made a considerable contribution to the decade of high growth from 1963 while the faltering contribution of manufacturing and construction since 1973 was reflected in the lower growth rate of GDP. This was the result of substantial structural change within manufacturing which experienced large contractions in output in real terms in 'traditional' sectors such as metal manufacture, shipbuilding and marine engineering after 1973. But there was considerable expansion, in real terms, in 'new' industries such as the food trades, chemicals, and instrument and electrical engineering. This process of restructuring continued in the 1980s with contraction in metal and mineral production, mechanical engineering, transport equipment and even the food trades, set against massive expansion in electrical and instrument engineering. A rather arbitrary division into traditional and new industries suggests that the former group contracted while the latter maintained a growth rate of 4 per cent between 1979 and 1988 suggesting a transformation to an industrial structure which promises better for the future, although throughout the 1980s the performance of all sectors was marked by a high level of volatility.

The further outstanding characteristic of structural change

Table 2 Scotland: weighted sectoral growth rates and GDP (per cent per annum)

		Agriculture	Energy/ Water	Manufac- turing	Construc- tion	Services	GDP
1951–60	A	0.07	0.01	0.61	0.21	0.65	1.55
1954–63	B	0.0	–0.04	0.48	0.31	–0.03	0.72
1963–73	B	0.14	0.11	1.02	0.28	1.51	3.05
1963–73	C	0.17	0.14	1.34	0.31	1.57	3.58
1973–79	B	–0.01	0.08	–0.22	–0.22	0.82	0.45
1973–79	C	–0.05	0.11	–0.29	–0.14	1.27	0.91
1979–88	C	0.11	0.05	0.16	–0.08	1.37	1.55
1954–79	B	0.06	0.06	0.54	0.14	0.91	1.71
1963–88	C	0.09	0.09	0.46	0.05	1.52	2.21

Sources: A: McCrone 1965: 35. B: Lythe and Majimudar 1982: 40–1. C: Scottish Office 1991, *Scottish Economic Bulletin* 43, p. 16.
Note: The weights used in the C series mean that the sectoral shares do not always sum exactly to the GDP growth figure.

since the 1950s has been the increasingly important role of the service sector, contributing over half the growth in the 1960s, all the growth in the 1970s recession including some compensation for decline in other sectors, and almost all the growth in the past decade. In common with most other advanced economies, in the twentieth century Scotland has become a service oriented economy for both production and employment. In the mid 1950s the Scottish service sector was rather different from the United Kingdom structure, with a marked orientation towards transport, and public services and a relative deficiency in distribution, finance and other services (Lythe and Majimudar 1982: 26). The service sector also performed poorly in the 1950s, with falling output in real terms in transport, public administration and defence, public health and education, and even financial services. In contrast the boom from the early 1960s until 1973 saw substantial real growth in every service sector and this continued through the 1970s with the exception of distribution. There was particularly high growth in public services. In the 1980s service sector growth was dominated by the financial sector although other subsectors achieved growth well above the rate of aggregate GDP. The growth of the financial sector reflected in some degree the effect of government deregulation, and the linked growth in range, quality and volume of financial services while the slower expansion of public services reflected another aspect of government policy. In any event the Scottish economy was clearly heavily reliant on services for continued growth by the end of the 1980s.

Employment and unemployment

The changes in the structure of production were mirrored, with variations caused by differences in productivity, in adjustments in the employment structure. Total employment in Scotland has remained very stable since the First World War, keeping within 2.5 per cent of 2.2 million people. But the overall stability conceals extensive changes in the composition of employment between economic sectors, between men and women, and between regions of Scotland. Agriculture, mining and many manufacturing industries have shed labour on a large scale so that employment in the non-service industries declined from just over one million jobs in 1901 to half that number by 1990 (Figure 6). Such a massive loss, within the context of a stable workforce, obviously required compen-

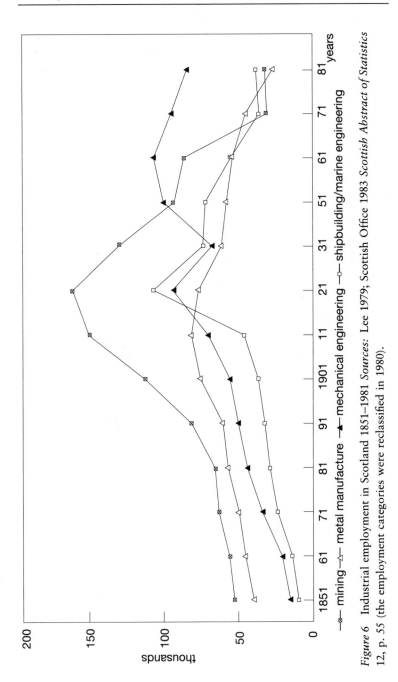

Figure 6 Industrial employment in Scotland 1851–1981 *Sources: Lee 1979; Scottish Office 1983 Scottish Abstract of Statistics* 12, p. 55 (the employment categories were reclassified in 1980).

—⊗— mining —△— metal manufacture —▲— mechanical engineering —□— shipbuilding/marine engineering satory expansion elsewhere. This has been primarily achieved in services where the massive expansion of employment in distributive trades, financial, professional and public services offset the decline in other services such as transport and domestic service as well as manufacturing. Much of this change has been concentrated into the past thirty years (Table 3).

These sectoral changes brought a substantial change in the balance of employment between the sexes. The Victorian economy relied on a male dominated workforce. Male employment in Scotland reached a peak just after the First World War at 1,570,000. Since then it has fallen so that by 1993 there were 993,000 males recorded as employees in employment, to which should be added perhaps another 150,000 self-employed and employers. But female employment moved sharply upward from under 600,000 at the beginning of the century to reach 800,000 in the early 1970s and 991,000 by 1993, an increase of almost 25 per cent in the past two decades (*Regional Trends* 29: 72). The share of women's employment has risen from 30 per cent of the Scottish total at the beginning of the century to close to 50 per cent by the 1990s, although some of this new employment has, of course, been in part-time jobs. The impact of restructuring, like the earlier growth which established the form of the economy at the beginning of the century, did not affect all regions of Scotland equally. In the half century from 1921 to 1971, employment fell in all regions other than Lothian and Central and Fife. The past two decades have seen a marked change in the substantial employment growth in Grampian, and to a lesser extent in the Highland region, while all other regions have continued to decline, sharply in the case of Strathclyde. Clearly the boom in the north east has prevented a substantial overall decline in the

Table 3 Employment in Scotland by sector (thousands)

Employment category	1901	1911	1921	1931	1951	1961	1971	1981	1993
0	238	228	219	199	162	128	88	44	27
1	135	164	198	162	126	116	67	73	53
2	72	92	124	109	123	119	104	67	36
3	158	193	288	214	276	277	281	215	154
4	430	422	419	414	372	317	309	229	175
5	146	115	68	101	151	173	177	141	108
6	153	166	266	331	272	317	278	385	414
7	152	183	160	177	181	174	144	129	110
8	17	23	30	33	33	42	63	129	204
9	338	351	435	451	497	533	645	590	703
NC	145	132	1	33	2	5	9	0	0
Total	1984	2069	2208	2224	2195	2201	2165	2002	1984

Sources: Lee 1979; Central Statistical Office Regional Trends 29, pp. 72–3.

Note: Estimates for 1981 and 1993 include employees in employment only.

Employment categories: 0: agricluture, forestry, fishing; 1: energy and water supply; 2: metals, minerals and chemicals; 3: metal goods, engineering, vehicles; 4: other manufacturing; 5: construction; 6: distribution, hotels/catering, repairs; 7: transport/communication; 8: banking, finance, insurance, business services, leasing; 9: public administration and other services; NC: not classified.

past twenty years.

Structural change has clearly been a painful process for many industries, regions and groups of workers in twentieth-century Scotland. The most visible and traumatic manifestation of that is seen in the unemployment figures. For Scotland as a whole unemployment stood at 16.1 per cent in 1931 in the depth of the interwar depression, a level similar to that in other industrial regions of the United Kingdom. Unemployment remained well above 100,000 throughout the interwar years, reaching 400,000 at the worst times (Leser 1954: 44). As unemployment rose again in the 1970s and 1980s, so Scottish rates were relatively but not uniquely high compared to other regions of the United Kingdom (Table 4). By 1991 unemployment stood at 220,000 people, an overall rate of 8.7 per cent in official statistics. This covered marked sex and regional variations, male unemployment standing at 11.5 per cent compared to 5.1 per cent for females. While male unemployment stood at 14.3 per cent in Strathclyde, and over ten per cent in Central, Fife and Tayside, in Grampian it was only 4.3 per cent (*Scotish Economic Bulletin* 45: 75). Overall regional unemployment rates ranged from 3. 7 per cent in Grampian to 10. 9 per cent in Strathclyde. While unemployment in Scotland has been sustained at high levels through much of the twentieth century, it has not been unusually high by comparison with other industrial areas of the United Kingdom with which it has shared a common experience of structural readjustment.

Between the wars, unemployment reflected a reduced level of demand, a situation which was reversed by preparation for war. But since 1945 the secular decline of heavy industry has wrought a massive restructuring and reduction in employment, especially on Clydeside, and this has increased unemployment. In the Clydeside conurbation employment fell from 844,000 in

Table 4 Regional unemployment rates (per cent)

	1931	1951	1954–63	1963/73	1973/79	1979/88	1988/93
South East	7.8	1.1	na	1.7	3.2	6.5	6.6
East Anglia	9.4	1.9	na	2.2	3.8	6.9	5.6
South West	8.1	1.8	na	2.7	5.1	7.8	6.7
West Midlands	12.1	1.3	na	2.1	4.5	10.8	8.4
East Midlands	9.6	1.2	na	2.1	3.9	8.3	7.2
North West	16.2	2.2	na	3.1	5.9	11.7	9.5
Yorkshire/ Humberside	12.2	1.6	na	2.7	4.6	10.3	8.7
North	19.2	3.1	2.7	4.9	7.1	13.4	10.6
Wales	16.5	3.5	3.1	4.1	6.3	11.6	8.9
Scotland	16.1	3.5	2.9	4.7	6.4	11.6	9.5
Northern Ireland	na	na	7.4	7.7	9.1	14.8	13.9
United Kingdom	na	na	1.8	2.8	4.8	9.1	8.1

Sources: Law 1980: 77; Central Statistical Office, 1965, *Abstract of Regional Statistics* 1, p. 9; Central Statistical Office, 1974, *Abstract of Regional Statistics* 10, p. 90; Central Statistical Office, 1982, *Regional Trends* 17, p. 109; Central Statistical Office, 1994, *Regional Trends* 29, p. 81.

1952 to 640,000 by 1984. These losses were particularly spectacular in Glasgow where work in manufacturing was cut by 50 per cent in the three decades after 1951 although this decline was exaggerated by the relocation of people under the overspill policy (Lever and Moore 1986: 2–4). In the rest of the conurbation total employment increased so there was both a restructuring effect in the shift from manufacturing to services and a locational effect in the shift away from the central city area. Since the traditional manufactures relied heavily on male manual employment these changes affected that group most severely. The annual average level of unemployment for men increased from 19,000 in Glasgow and 10,000 in the rest of the conurbation in the 1960s to 54,000 and 51,000 respectively by the mid 1980s. Even these figures underestimate the extent of the change, since they omit those leaving the labour market altogether, changes in the measurement of unemployment in the 1980s, and the existence of employment programmes which remove individuals from the register. Strathclyde Regional Council estimated that in 1984 the recorded unemployment figures of 105,000 males and 42,000 females should be augmented by 20,000 excluded by definitional changes, 26,000 unemployed but unregistered, and 37,000 absorbed into employment schemes (Lever and Moore 1986: 29). In Glasgow in the 1980s, the number of long-term male unemployed, who had been out of work for two years or more, increased rapidly. In 1985 it was estimated that 5,000 of Glasgow's male unemployed had not worked for five years. In the rest of the conurbation there was considerable variation with black spots of industrial decline recording high levels of unemployment, as in Monklands where the rate was 22.0 per cent and Clydebank where it was 20.8 per cent although much lower levels were found in the new towns. The recession of the late 1970s and early 1980s spread unemployment to the outer urban areas, exacerbated by the fact that they had an increasing supply of labour. In Glasgow the fundamental problem lay in the long-term unemployed, a group which always finds difficulty in rejoining the labour market even in a time of recovery. In 1991 the average male unemployment rate in Strathclyde stood at 14.6 per cent which represented over 93,000 men out of work, over half the total in Scotland. Fife, Central and Tayside with similar histories of industrial decline shared high male unemployment rates of over 10 per cent.

The persistently high levels of unemployment in large areas

of central Scotland indicate the difficulties occasioned by the extensive contraction of major employment sectors and of replacing such jobs with new work. A further manifestation of this decline, although it tends to amelioration of the immediate problem has been the steady stream of migration from Scotland, a sustained net outward flow of migrants at the average rate of 250,000 per decade over the past century although it reached 392,000 in the 1920s and 325,000 in the 1960s, a total loss of over two million people (Law 1980: 60). This has contributed to the declining rate of population growth although there was an overall increase from four to five millions between the 1890s and the 1990s. But the Scottish population has been declining slightly since the early 1970s (Figure 1). The main constituents of this change are quite clear. The birth rate has followed a downward path since the beginning of the century, a trend which was temporarily reversed after the two world wars and in the early 1960s, but which has been characterised by sharp decline in recent decades. The other half of the equation of natural increase, the death rate, fell rapidly until the 1920s since when it has stabilised. The conjunction of these two forces has produced a convergence in the birth and death rates so that the rate of natural increase has actually fallen. Indeed, in the past twenty years they have been almost in balance, indicating a stable population. The loss of population through migration, added to this balance of natural forces, explains the absolute fall in the Scottish population during the past two decades so that it currently stands at a similar level to 1950 at 5.1 million people.

The changing pattern of population growth has brought a substantial shift in the age composition of the Scottish population. Falling birth rates and outward migration have reduced the proportion of young people under fifteen years of age from

33.4 per cent of the population in 1901 to 24.6 per cent in 1951 and a projected 19.1 per cent by 2001. At the other end of the scale, those over 65 years of age have become a substantially larger share of the population, increasing from 4.9 per cent at the beginning of the century to 9.9 per cent in 1951 and a projected 15.7 per cent by the end of the century. Overall the population has aged substantially in the course of the twentieth century, and while the proportion of those of working age, 15 to 64, has increased slightly, it too has shifted in favour of the higher age groups.

Wealth, income and welfare

The extensive structural change in production and employment experienced in the twentieth century had widespread ramifications on the affluence of the Scottish people and included both substantial benefits and costs. On the credit side is the fact that during the course of the twentieth century both aggregate national income and income per head have grown substantially, and in the 1950s and 1960s at a historically unprecedented rate. Within that context both wealth and income have become more equitably distributed. This has been the result not of actual redistribution away from the most affluent, but a relative loss as other groups in society have increased their income and wealth at a relatively faster rate, principally as a result of becoming home owners. Thus while the share of the top 10 per cent of wealth holders in the United Kingdom fell from 92 per cent to 61 per cent of the national total between 1911/13 and 1976, since total wealth increased from £6 billion to £274 billion between these dates, the gain of the most favoured ten per cent was 60 per cent of the net increase. Wealth distribution estimates for Scotland are less abundant. But the Royal Commission on the distribution of wealth found that in 1973 the top 5 per cent of Scots held 30.6 per cent of the national wealth compared to 22.8 per cent in England and Wales while the top 10 per cent enjoyed 79.3 and 66.1 per cent respectively. Furthermore, only one third of adult Scots were identified as wealth holders compared to half the adults in England and Wales (Royal Commission Cmd 6171: 123).

Income, which is almost invariably more equally distributed than wealth, showed the same trend over time for the United Kingdom , the share of the top 10 per cent falling from 39 per cent in the late 1930s to 26 per cent by the mid 1970s (Lee 1986: 147). This relative redistribution of income was to the benefit of the middle income groups, those in the bottom 30–40 per cent making little gain. Both the trends towards greater equality in the distribution of wealth and income are the result of growing middle class affluence in the acquisition of property and better remunerated employment, as well as higher activity rates resulting from increasing job oppportunities for women since 1945.

The structure of these income estimates provides important indicators for the explanation of relative performance. Several analyses of the Scottish data have identified a number of characteristics which have remained influential since the 1920s. The interwar year estimates suggested relatively low earnings in Scotland with an especially small proportion of salary earners, some four per cent less than the national average (Campbell 1954: 52–4). Conversely, property income was relatively more important in Scotland, indicating more farmers, more small businesses and a skewed income distribution. Unemployment and traditionally low wages were also canvassed as explanatory variables (Campbell 1955: 234–5). A later survey, taken in 1959/60, found the same pattern. Wages and salaries in Scotland remained more than 10 per cent below the national average although profits and professional earnings were above the average. A similar pattern was indicated by the income assessed for tax data (McCrone 1965: 78, 80).

Recent estimates confirm the enduring pattern. The distribution of income liable to taxation in 1987/88 showed Scotland far above the United Kingdom average (25.0 per cent against 19.9 per cent) for incomes below £5,000 per year, the highest share of any region. At the other extreme, Scotland fell below the United Kingdom average for all incomes over £10,000 per annum. There were also large variations within Scotland, especially in terms of male weekly earnings. While Grampian stood far above the British average in 1991 (£364 against £319) Scotland as a whole fell well below it (£300) and some regions did particularly poorly, Dumfries and Galloway £268, Tayside £279 and Fife £285 (*Scottish Economic Bulletin* 44: 76).

The economics of structural decline has meant that the traditional low wages earned in the shipyards and steel works have been replaced by the modest incomes afforded by state benefits. But the widespread growth of those dependent on social security payments is another reflection of enduring poverty. By 1989 almost half a million people in Scotland were receiving income support. Two other changes compounded this dependence on the state. The principal impact on social security expenditure has been the number of persons surviving well beyond working age and thus claiming retirement pensions. The number of people in Scotland over the age of 64 increased from 219,000 at the beginning of the century to reach 765,000 by 1991, an increase from 5 to 15 per cent of the total population. The number claiming pensions shot up from 497,000 in 1961 to 780,000 in 1989 (*Scottish Abstract of Statis-*

tics 19: 14). By the end of the 1980s retirement pensions accounted for 38. 7 per cent of all social security payments and was the largest single item in that account. The main social determinants of growing demands on social security funds reflect several causal strands in family poverty. The increase in the number of single parent families, unemployment and the prevalence of part-time work for women together drove up demands on supplementary benefit, and income support which replaced it in 1988. This was paid to those who were not in full time employment but whose income fell below a defined minimum. The number of persons receiving supplementary benefit in Scotland increased from 190,000 in 1961 to 535,000 by 1987, substantial growth being generated in the 1980s. The category of claimants defined as 'unemployed without contributory benefits' provided much of this expansion increasing from 10 per cent of recipients in 1961 to 40 per cent by 1987 (*Scottish Abstract of Statistics* 1: 13; 19: 18–19). The effect of all such changes has been to generate a massive demand for social security payments in Scotland, as elsewhere in the United Kingdom, by almost 50 per cent in the 1980s alone.

One of the most obvious indicators of relative prosperity or deprivation is provided by health statistics. The adjusted age mortality rates for 1989 showed that Scotland had the worst record in the United Kingdom. Males suffered 205 deaths per 100,000 population above the national average and females suffered 199 deaths above it. In most major identified causes, including heart disease, cancer, cerebrovascular disease, and peumonia Scotland did very badly in comparison with the rest of the country and was distinctly worse than Northern Ireland which came next in this unhappy list (*Regional Trends* 26: 117).

The poor health record of Scotland was apparent between

the wars and earlier. It is by no means a modern development as a memorandum sent to the cabinet by the Scottish Secretary in 1937 shows:

> The social condition of Scotland is indicated by the fact that 23% of its population live in conditions of gross overcrowding compared with 4% in England ... Until 25 years ago the infant mortality rate in Scotland was lower than in England, but since then the Scottish rate has fallen more slowly than in England which it now exceeds by 35%. Maternal mortality is half as high again as in England. In proportion to the population twice as many cases of pneumonia and of scarlet fever were notified ... while the diphtheria figure was higher by a third (Levitt 1983: 72).

There were also significant regional variations in the incidence of illness in Scotland. Tuberculosis was greatest in the Highlands, Strathclyde and the major cities, other than Edinburgh, while infant mortality was worst on Clydeside, Glasgow having the worst rate in the United Kingdom.

Ill health in Scotland reflects the concentration of poor people. Much of the Clydeside area has centres of multiple deprivation which generate high mortality levels. A study of perinatal deaths in Glasgow in 1970 showed a close correlation between the death rate and the social class distribution with environmental factors playing a major role. Similarly a study of Inverclyde and Renfrew identified poor housing, unemployment, financial difficulties, large families and smoking as influences on the rate of infant and perinatal mortality (Hubley 1983: 214). Many of the diseases which appear to achieve greater success in Scotland than elsewhere reflect poor housing and sanitation, like tuberculosis, or indulgence like smoking, linked to lung cancer and heart disease, and drinking, linked to cirrhosis of the liver. Even the escape routes from deprivation entail a high health cost.

Scotland has long had a history of chronic ill health, sustaining death rates from heart disease and lung cancer amongst the highest in the world as well as a relatively high infant mortality rate. But the really significant variations are those between social groups, semi-skilled and unskilled manual workers being far more susceptible than professional or managerial personnel and their families. The lung cancer registration rates in Scotland for 1972–74 for male professional workers was 740 cases per 100,000 population, compared to 2,888 for manual workers, while the infant mortality rates suffered by the same groups were 9.2 and 21.5 respectively (Hubley 1983: 209).

Such a society is locked, by a variety of mechanisms, into a cycle of decline. In a period of increasing pressure on state spending, and given an administration committed to private rather than public initiative, sustained efforts to curtail such benefits must be expected. This, in turn, will further curtail the spending power of the national and local economy and deficient effective demand has long been a severe restraint on the growth of Scottish economy. This was probably the most significant and baleful legacy from Victorian industrialisation. The low wages which gave Scottish industry a comparative advantage over its southern competitors, entailed a resultant modest rate of spending which restrained effective demand for consumer goods and services. Scotland's long-term poor record in employment in both these areas is indicative of this. As a result the self-sustaining process whereby high incomes and a relatively high level of employment sustain and expand demand, thus creating more jobs and demand in a virtuous circle of expansion as demonstrated in south east England, was always much weaker in Scotland. In turn this makes the transition from one economic structure to another even more difficult and painful to achieve. The economic history of twentieth century Scotland has been dominated by the pressures forcing the contraction of established industries and those promising regeneration through new activities.

Chapter 4

The economics of decline

Demand, recession and competition

Much of the recent academic literature on the Scottish economy has been concerned with the pathology of industrial
decline, especially with the failing giants of Victorian industry,
coal, iron and steel, heavy engineering and shipbuilding, all of
which were clustered in the central belt between the Clyde and
the Forth. Their historical experience followed a clearly
defined pattern of growth and decline in the twentieth century,
boosted by the two world wars and the postwar boom of the
1950s, depressed in the interwar years recession and increasingly in difficulty from the 1960s onwards.

Prior to the First World War, British shipbuilding enjoyed
substantial expansion and domination in international markets, although heavy industry has always been susceptible to
considerable fluctuations in demand, and not least when
dependent on exports. The First World War offered a new
stimulus as 30 per cent of the pre-war merchant fleet of the
entire world was lost in the conflict. The anticipated replacement boom provided the context for the frantic expansion and
attempts to control inputs like steel, but the British were not
alone in contributing to the massive increase in world mer-

cantile tonnage in the early 1920s as the United States, Japan, Holland and Sweden greatly increased their capacity. In the event, world trade grew far more fitfully than had been expected and, in the 1930s, slumped dramatically. Throughout the interwar period the world shipbuilding industry faced a state of massive excess productive capacity so that world output fell from its peak of six million tons in 1920 to an average of two million per year between 1924 and 1938. British yards alone had a capacity of three million tons, and were effectively confined to domestic demand as their competitors were helped by various types of government assistance (Payne 1992: 31). Further the lucrative naval contracts which had contributed 15 per cent of tonnage launched from British yards in the decade before the war did not reappear on a significant scale until the later 1930s. The interwar years were thus characterised by a prolonged depression in effective demand for shipping. Tonnage lauched on the Clyde fell from 676,000 tons in 1911–13 to 293,000 tons in 1935–37, helped by the fact that its yards specialised in those sectors, liners and warships, for which demand remained least depressed (Slaven 1975: 184). But some specialist east coast yards fared quite well; the Burntisland Shipbuilding Company, for example, was a successful manufacturer of coal carriers.

The Clyde, like other rivers, was revived by rearmament in the 1930s. Admiralty contracts had been a significant source of demand for some Clydeside yards since the late nineteenth century, about 45 per cent of the tonnage ordered in the quarter century before 1914 and a similar share of wartime orders were of this kind (Peebles 1987: 1–2). Naval work comprised half the value of all shipping built at Clydebank in the 1930s. The revival of military orders also provided Beardmore with a decade of prosperous business after 1932. The boost of naval contracts enabled some firms to keep abreast with the latest technology. In the depths of the depression the John Brown yard had half its berths equipped with ten-ton cranes and welding capacity installed for prefabrication work (Slaven 1977: 213).

The Great War had provided a welcome boost to Scottish steel manufacture with a doubling of output compared to the 1900s, although it also revealed the technical weakness of the Scottish industry. Prior to the war acid steel, preferred by the shipyards as stronger and more reliable than basic steel, dominated Scottish production. Military requirements prevailed so that basic steel increased from under 20 per cent of Scottish steel output in 1913 to 75 per cent by the late 1930s, an increase by over 1.1 million tons (Buxton 1976: 109). Between the wars demand for steel was both erratic and relatively depressed (Figure 7). It has been estimated that Clydeside and Belfast shipyards took 60 per cent of Scottish steel between the wars, and most of the steel manufacturers were linked in some way with the shipbuilding industry. For those without such contacts, even in the context of the depressed shipyards, markets could be even harder to secure. Beardmore struggled with a variety of manufactures in the 1920s, but only armour and steel forging avoided losses. The firm's fortunes improved most obviously with the revival in 1932 of an armour pool under Admiralty pressure in which it was joined by Firth Brown and English Steel. Since Beardmore had previously not had any orders, its 25 per cent share was most welcome, especially when the increase of the pool in 1936 doubled production (Hume and Moss 1979: 240). Rearmament restored demand for steel in the 1930s.

The slump in the fortunes of heavy industry between the wars could be written off, with some justification, to depres-

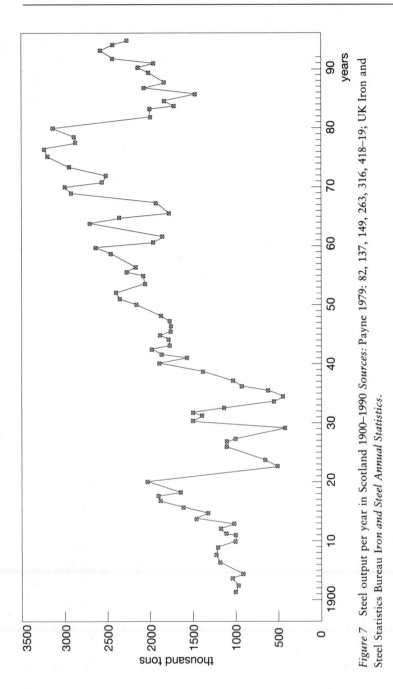

Figure 7   Steel output per year in Scotland 1900–1990 *Sources:* Payne 1979: 82, 137, 149, 263, 316, 418–19; UK Iron and Steel Statistics Bureau *Iron and Steel Annual Statistics*.

sion in world markets. Typically the coal industry suffered from falling export demand as European competitors protected their domestic producers. It also suffered from the depression throughout heavy industry for which coal was the principal fuel as well as from the increased efficiency in the use of coal in manufacturing. By then the industry was embarked on a long road of secular decline (Figure 2). Difficulties were also partly concealed or deferred by the stimulus afforded by the two world wars. But increasingly since the 1940s, the decline of heavy industry has reflected a weakness in competition in the context of expanding, albeit changing, international markets. This was spectacularly true of shipbuilding (Figure 8). Britain's share of the world market fell from 35 per cent of tonnage launched in 1948–50 to 4.5 per cent between 1961–65. This was followed by the loss of the home market from 81.1 per cent of tonnage in 1956–60 to 26.0 per cent ten years later (Lorenz and Wilkinson 1986: 116–17). Mercantile tonnage launched on the Clyde fell from 442,000 in 1950 to 323,000 by the time of nationalisation in 1977. Thereafter the decline was far sharper reaching 190,000 in 1982 (Payne 1985: 107). By the end of the 1980s Scottish mercantile shipping tonnage completed was less than 5 per cent of the output level sustained throughout the 1950s. But world shipbuilding production soared in these postwar decades, mercantile tonnage launched increasing tenfold between 1950 and the peak of the mid 1970s.

Scottish steel production enjoyed an upward if erratic trend in output from the Second World War until the early 1970s. In part this reflected the trends in shipbuilding, but the relationship was far weaker than between the wars. It also reflected an element of oversupply which was eventually exposed. Recurrent anxieties were voiced in the 1950s and 1960s about

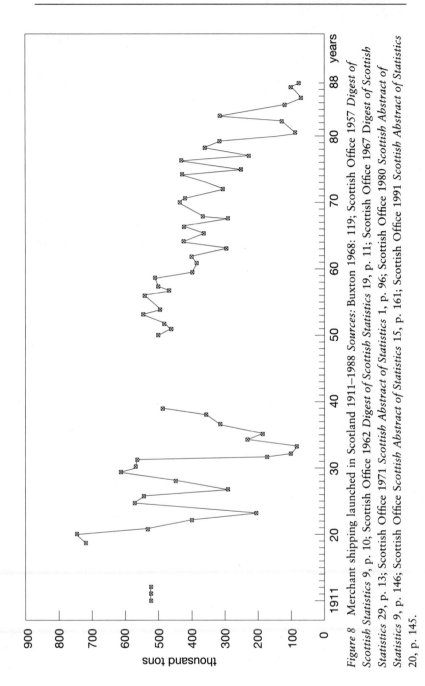

Figure 8 Merchant shipping launched in Scotland 1911–1988 *Sources:* Buxton 1968: 119; Scottish Office 1957 *Digest of Scottish Statistics* 9, p. 10; Scottish Office 1962 *Digest of Scottish Statistics* 19, p. 11; Scottish Office 1967 *Digest of Scottish Statistics* 29, p. 13; Scottish Office 1971 *Scottish Abstract of Statistics* 1, p. 96; Scottish Office 1980 *Scottish Abstract of Statistics* 15, p. 161; Scottish Office 1991 *Scottish Abstract of Statistics* 20, p. 145.

the weak demand for steel in Scotland. The industry lacked facilities to produce the sheet metal and light plates required in consumer durables and the motor industry, and sales of steel outside Scotland were hampered by the constraint of high freight charges inflating price in competitive markets. Sustained demand for Scottish steel came to be increasingly reliant on government intervention, both in creating a market by relocating industrial consumers as well as by direct aid to production through other grants and subsidies.

The slump in the demand for coal which occurred in the late 1950s presaged a fundamental shift in demand for fuel. Prior to that time, coal enjoyed a virtual monopoly of the home market for energy, 1956 being the peak year for consumption. Thereafter, in common with much of the rest of the world, British consumers, industrial and domestic, switched to electricity, oil and gas. Some changes were dramatically swift. Railway consumption fell from 14.7 million tons per year in 1950 to 0.6 million tons by 1967–68 as diesel and electricity replaced steam. Total British consumption fell from 221 million tons in 1956 to 120 million tons by 1980–81. This would have been even greater had the electricity generating power stations not more than doubled their demand, so that by the 1980s they comprised over 70 per cent of the total demand for coal (Ashworth 1986: 38–42). Effective demand thus depended on the state, the government insisting that the power stations use coal, not always their cheapest or preferred fuel. The final prop to the industry was removed with the privatisation of electricity supply and the removal of the industry's obligation to use domestically produced coal. The result of this collapse in demand for coal, in Scotland, was a fall in output between 1951 and 1989 from 23.6 million to 2.1 million tons, and a commensurate drop in employment in mining from 82,200 to about 4,000.

The weight of tradition: structure and organisation

The problems of variable demand in increasingly competitive international markets were compounded by the fact that heavy industry in Scotland and the rest of the United Kingdom was inhibited in the effectiveness of its response by organisation structures evolved and crystallised in an era of small scale production. Shipbuilding, like many other long established industries, had evolved a structure suitable to its early expansive phase. There were many small firms, most of them under family ownership and control. Between the wars over 100 firms operated as shipbuilders in Scotland alone. On the Clyde in 1938 there were 32 shipbuilding and marine engineering firms, 22 of which were private limited companies (Slaven 1982: 35). Few firms specialised in a single type of vessel, of which 73 categories were recognised, but built to particular specifications. Each shipyard was divided into several departments which marked the progression of construction. John Brown of Clydebank had no less than 19 separate departments. As a result, a key management task lay in co-ordinating the flow of work through the system. In buoyant market conditions this system possessed the flexibility to undertake such tasks effectively, to respond to market change, and to sustain efficient working.

But the depressed demand conditions which prevailed between the wars revealed the limitations of this established structure when under stress. The irregular nature of demand provided an inherent tendency towards overcapacity in the industry. Tight schedules for delivery induced overmanning and the retention of a wide range of berth sizes, all of which contributed to a high capital/earnings ratio.

The cost problem impinged immediately on the shipbuilder's

ability to obtain new orders, and completed a cycle of linked circumstances which debilitated the industry between the wars. Weak demand made for a poor order book which meant a low level of capacity utilisation. Low load factors increased over-heads and raised production costs. High levels of costs con-tributed to high prices and poor competitiveness, which made it even more difficult for a company to obtain a share of the few orders available in the market place (Slaven 1977: 194).

The limitations of the system under conditions of depressed demand were equally restrictive when the market expanded after 1945. The massive increase in world demand for ship-ping, and new types of vessel, brought substantial changes in production methods. Oil tankers were typical of the new and very large vessels which could be made from large standard components welded together. The development of welding and prefabrication techniques made possible large scale production and made the keel-based tradition of manufacture outmoded. The new methods required massive assembly areas with large cranes to manipulate the prefabricated sections into position. Traditional craft skills were supplanted by semi-skilled assem-bly. 'In general, competitive performance in shipbuilding now depended less on having a skilled workforce sufficiently versa-tile to produce complex vessels to customer specifications, and more on producers' ability to expand the scale of their yards, standardise their production, and provide for effective man-agerial co-ordination of production from above (Lorenz and Wilkinson 1986: 118–19). Such a transformation ran counter to the traditions of British yards and the vested interests of both the shipbuilders and their skilled craftsmen.

Most British yards, including those on the Clyde, had little room for physical expansion. They also had a substantial investment in outmoded but still usable equipment, while the tradition of rivalry precluded collusive reallocation of work between yards. Nor was any firm big enough to absorb rivals through merger, while the government, unlike its French counterpart in the 1960s, did not force amalgamation and rationalisation. Nor were the notoriously poor labour relations helpful to modernisation as specialist skilled craft groups sought to maintain their pay differentials and other privileges. When the industry was nationalised in 1977, there were 168 separate bargaining agreements in force.

Historically long established structures restricted the competitiveness of the iron and steel industry. Production expansion during the First World War revealed the inadequacy of Scottish pig iron output, operating on an extremely small scale, and close to exhausting its supply of indigenous raw materials. As a consequence it was unable to match the expansion of steel production and the ratio of Scottish pig iron to steel fell from 37 per cent to 7 per cent between 1913–38, leaving the industry with a seriously imbalanced production chain. The shortfall was made up by imports of pig iron from England, Europe and India and an increasing use of scrap. By the 1930s twice as much scrap as pig iron was used in the production of Scottish steel. Coking coal was another source of resource shortage, and by the 1930s it was insufficient to supply the demands of the modest and shrinking Scottish pig iron industry, falling over 25 per cent short of demand. The north east of England made up most of the shortfall. It was also much cheaper, even when transport costs were included. Scottish coke oven plants were small and antiquated and had difficulty in selling by-products like gas. Glasgow Corporation, for example, refused an offer of supply.

The resource limitations and structural weaknesses increased costs, as did the unfavourable location of the Scottish industry in central Lanarkshire while the balance of advantage had shifted to coastal locations to reduce transport costs in an industry where inputs and outputs were expensive to move. The cost of delivering steel for export to the Clyde from Lanarkshire was more than double the cost incurred by some of their English competitors in the 1920s in transporting steel to the ports. The dispersed and disjointed process of production also added to costs. This was especially true of the antiquated 'cold-metal' practice whereby pig iron was allowed to go cold and had to be reheated before transformation into steel. When the 'hot-metal' practice was introduced in the late 1930s at the Clyde Iron Works and Clydebridge Steelworks, although they were separated by the river, it cut steel production costs by 10 per cent (Buxton 1976: 115). Not surprisingly, discussion about integrated production and relocation to the coast loomed large in rationalisation schemes. One major Scottish producer found a more radical solution, Stewart and Lloyd moving from the Mossend works to Corby in the east midlands, a location close to cheap ironstone supplies, the midland and southern markets, and in which productive processes could be fully integrated. Other companies might also have been tempted to move south had it not been for their ties with the shipbuilders.

By the end of the 1920s the problems of Scottish steel had become sufficiently serious to secure agreement amongst the main producers, and the largest iron manufacturer, for the commissioning of a report on the industry by a leading American engineering consultant H. A. Brassert & Co. This report concluded that the traditional splint coal blast furnace technology was now obsolete and that modern best practice required a fully integrated production process from iron ore to finished steel. The report thus proposed the construction of a new fully integrated iron and steel works with coke oven plant on the Clyde near Erskine Ferry. It also rejected redevelopment on the basis of any existing site. Several explanations have been offered for the industry's rejection of the scheme. Payne (1979) has emphasised the personal antipathies between the steel masters. Tolliday has stressed economic considerations, in the failure of the report to consider current market conditions and the assumption that scrap would become more expensive, thus warranting the expansion of Scottish pig iron output. All these factors allowed the industry to argue that the cost savings identified by Brassert would be less than projected, paring down the proposed saving of £1.2 million to less than £160,000 (Tolliday 1987: 105).

The rejection of plans for rationalisation of production ensured that the weaknesses which appeared in the Scottish steel industry between the wars remained after 1945. The possibility of implementing the Brassert Report recommendations was again raised in the late 1940s. It had played no part in the development plan submitted by Colvilles to the Iron and Steel Federation in 1944, which had been a conservative document concerned to maintain the current level of productive capacity, but concentrated into larger units of production without causing social dislocation by shifting location or closing plants (Payne 1979: 279). When the Brassert scheme was raised, Colvilles flatly rejected it, refusing to admit that a new works would cut production costs, and rejecting the implicit assumption that demand for steel would increase. In the event steel production was higher than in the interwar years, reaching a peak in the late 1960s at a little over three million tons per annum (Payne 1979: 316, 418). The plan reappeared again after the 1967 nationalisation when the new regional division of British Steel which embraced Scotland and the north west of England proposed constructing an ore terminal at Hunterston on the Clyde capable of handling vessels of up to 200,000 tons and a fully integrated iron and steel works on an adjacent site with a productive capacity of five to six million tons. In 1973 work started on the ore and coal terminal for vessels up to 35,000 tons and was completed five years later together with two Midrex direct reduction plants intended to bring the most modern iron manufacturing methods to Scotland (Payne 1985: 97). But rapid increases in natural gas prices meant that the two units were never operational and the plan to construct electric arc furnaces, which the direct reduction plant was intended to supply, was abandoned.

The final failure of the coastal location strategy consolidated Scottish production in central Lanarkshire with all the historical disadvantages that entailed. The restoration of the geographical divisional structure in the British Steel Corporation (BSC) in the 1970s revealed the relatively high costs of Scottish production. In the later 1970s, as demand declined, losses per ton were far higher in Scotland than in any of the other divisions of BSC and in some years were greater than all the others combined (Payne 1985: 100). This reflected the smaller scale of production, a lower proportion of capacity utilised, plus higher fuel and transport costs. Output per blast furnace in 1990 in Scotland was only 67.5 per cent of the British average. Only political pressure prevented closure in the 1980s, although privatisation of the industry in 1988 marked the final death knell for steel production in Scotland. Employment in the industry in 1991 stood at 2,600, less than 10 per cent of its 1974 level, and half of that number was employed at Ravenscraig which subsequently closed in 1992 despite the fact that, by then, the plant had achieved considerable productivity gains and closed much of the gap between itself and other districts.

The problems caused by a declining resource base were compounded by another aspect of the historical legacy. In the coal industry this took the form of dispersed ownership of mineral rights and the large number of small undertakings. Buxton (1970) has argued, against the conventional wisdom, that small scale production was not a disadvantage in the interwar years, citing the large number of small Scottish pits and the high relative productivity levels achieved in Scotland by mechanisation. But Scottish pits, as a survey taken in 1935 showed, included a higher than average output from small workings of under 100,000 tons per annum, as well as from very large workings of over two million tons per annum than the British average, which casts some doubt on this conclusion (Supple 1987: 373). Historians of the more recent past have compared the small scale of Scottish operations unfavourably with larger coalfields in Yorkshire and the east midlands. Certainly Scottish productivity remained stuck some 15 per cent below the industry average through the 1960s and 1970s, a factor which has been explained by the large number of support workers needed to supplement those at the coalface (Payne 1985: 89).

Solutions: merger and nationalisation

The increasingly harsh economic environment faced by heavy industry in the twentieth century brought a number of characteristic responses as a means of ameliorating that situation. Industry solutions primarily consisted of collusive action or merger as a means of securing control of the market. Increasingly as the century progressed and the problems became more urgent, the government became involved in assisting or imposing rationalisation. The favoured mechanism for ensuring a flow of orders in shipbuilding was the 'builders' friend' manifest through the operation of overlapping directorships. Lord Pirrie, the most famous, held six chairmanships and 27 directorships at the end of the First World War. The harsh competitive environment of the interwar years diminished the effectiveness of such links, leading to increasingly competitive tendering often resulting in losses (Slaven 1977: 198). For the first time the industry recognised that concerted action was essential. The Shipbuilding Conference established in 1928 provided a pool of confidential information to which members supplied data relevant to tenders to determine the minimal acceptable conditions. In 1930 the National Shipbuilders Security Ltd was established to finance the closure of yards as a way of reducing excess capacity paid for by a 1 per cent levy on all new orders. Under this scheme 19 per cent of the shipbuilding capacity of the Clyde was eliminated.

The problems of shipbuilding between the wars heavily influenced the steel industry as the result both of a long-established reliance on its demand for steel and as a result of a series of mergers engineered in the early 1920s. Anticipating a post-war boom for shipping, and fearing a steel shortage which would curb their response to that market opportunity, the shipbuilders sought to protect their supplies through the purchase of steel manufacturers. Some firms, like the Steel Company of Scotland were bought by a consortium of Clydeside shipbuilders, while control of Colvilles was acquired by Harland and Wolff of Belfast. While there were a spate of such take-overs after the First World War such links were not a novelty. John Brown & Co was originally a Sheffield steel and armour plate manufacturer which extended into shipbuilding with the purchase of the Clydebank yard in 1899. The company also had links with another Clydeside shipyard, Fairfield, with Cammell Laird and the Coventry Ordnance Works. John Brown later resolved a financial crisis by merging with Thomas Firth, another Sheffield steel manufacturer. Beardmore joined with the Tyneside shipbuilders Swan Hunter and Wigham Richardson to purchase the Glasgow Iron and Steel Company. Heavy industry in the west of Scotland was closely bound to shipbuilding, steel and armament manufacturers elsewhere, especially in Belfast, Sheffield and the north east of England. In the depth of the depression a substantial 37 per cent of Clydebridge ship plate was sold by Colvilles to Harland and Wolff and John Brown. Beardmore, without such links, had difficulty securing orders for its plate mill. When P & O commissioned two large steamships in the 1920s the contract stipulated that steel should be purchased from those firms associated with the purchaser rather than those linked to the supplier, as was the usual convention. The two largest and most capital intensive industries in Clydeside and Northern Ireland were thus concentrated in massive vertically integrated combines.

In addition to the difficulties which steel firms inherited from their shipbuilding associates, many had also accumulated substantial debts by the 1920s. Throughout that decade Colvilles had an overdraft in excess of £500, 000 with the National Bank of Scotland, while the Steel Company of Scotland was heavily indebted to the Royal Exchange Assurance. The problems of the steel industry thus focused attention on some type of rationalisation and restructuring in which there were several interested parties, including the steelmakers, the shipbuilders, the banks and, in due course, the government. By the mid 1920s Beardmore had debts of £3 million greater than the value of the liquid assets of the company, and had difficulty in securing further credit from its bankers. In 1929 the Bank of England provided £750,000 to keep the company working and retained control until 1938.

The possibility of relocating Scottish steel production at a coastal location had been tentatively considered even before 1914. Lord Weir's scheme, put forward in the late 1920s, offered large cost savings amounting to 25 per cent in both pig iron and finished steel (Buxton 1976: 114). But there was little enthusiasm amongst steel producers for either heavy investment at a time of recession or restructuring which might inhibit their individual independence. Nor in the 1920s were shipbuilders supportive of such moves, fearing a rise in steel prices. The banks also hampered mergers when their own resources were at risk. Lloyds Bank had a large shareholding in the Lanarkshire Steel Company in the 1920s and prevented the sale of that company to Colvilles at a price which would incur losses (Tolliday 1987: 94).

The rejection of any radical solution to the problems of the industry left merger as the only route towards rationalisation. In the 1930s the Bank of England increased pressure for merger, supported now by the shipbuilding interests led by Sir James Lithgow who used his massive financial resources to engineer the process of amalgamation. With his brother Henry, he was reported to have made a profit of £283,000 from this. The sum was subsequently donated to the pension fund for ministers of the Church of Scotland, and other religious causes like the Iona Community although the Lithgows did not approve of George Macleod's activities. As a result Colvilles emerged by 1936 in control of 80 per cent of Scottish steel production. This included the Stewart and Lloyd plate business, the Mossend works of Beardmore, the Steel Company of Scotland and the Lanarkshire Steel Company. But the concentration of ownership and control did not extend to rationalisation of production. The new combine simply continued to extemporise within the existing framework of production with little new investment, remaining heavily dependent on scrap, having only a single hot-metal steelworks by the end of the 1930s, and modernising within the old locations. Hence the critical judgement of Tolliday that the rationalisation process was a sham.

Pressures towards merger reappeared in the postwar period. Clydeside yards faced increasing disadvantages from the 1950s compared to the mixture of tax relief, low interest rates, subsidies and credits offered by government to their overseas competitors. By the early 1960s famous names were beginning to disappear from the river and in 1965 the major Fairfield yard was declared bankrupt. Towards the end of that decade several mergers were arranged, forming Scott Lithgow in 1967 and the Upper Clyde Shipbuilders in 1968, including Fairfield, John Brown, Charles Connell, Yarrow and Stephen while yards in Dundee, Burntisland and Leith formed Robb Caledon. Government funds were needed to offset the effects of injudicious tendering, inflation and rising wage costs. By 1971 Upper Clyde Shipbuilders had disappeared to re-emerge as Govan Shipbuilders although its capacity to absorb public subsidies remained unabated, £80 million having been spent by 1976 (Payne 1985: 106). In 1972 Marathon bought the John Brown yard, backed by public subventions, and converted it to oil platform production. By the time the industry was taken into public ownership it was in the usually half-hearted fashion.

Forty-odd companies, in various stages of decay, had been brought together in 1977 with no common financial system, plan or organisational structure and, although attempts were made by senior management to create a viable centralised structure, each company management retained its own ideas about what to do. The situation had been described as the beginning of 'guerilla warfare between subsidiaries and the centre' (Strath 1987: 132).

By 1979–80 half the £110 million losses incurred by the nationalised British Shipbuilders were attributed to Scottish yards, Scott Lithgow contributing a substantial share. Losses and redundancies continued through the 1980s as decline accelerated.

The increasing role of the state in shipbuilding rationalisation, from the oblique influence of the Treasury and the Bank of England in the 1920s to the appearance of nationalised companies and eventually full scale nationalisation of the industry in the more recent past marked a pattern of state involvement which extended to steel and coal. By the early 1950s Britain had three continuous steel strip mills, and there was general acceptance in industrial and political circles that a fourth was needed. The best site on economic grounds was Immingham on Humberside, but there was a strong Welsh and Scottish political lobby for sites with justification offered on social grounds. The Scottish case was advanced by John Maclay, the Secretary of State for Scotland, and Iain Macleod, the Minister of Labour, on the basis of the need to create economic growth and Scotland's falling share of United Kingdom steel output. Colvilles were approached, but the firm's lack of enthusiasm is clearly revealed by Sir Andrew McCance's memorandum on his meeting with the Secretary of State:

Mr Maclay asked whether Colvilles would be embarrassed if it were decided to [insist that Richard Thomas & Baldwins] build the strip mill in Scotland and what would be our attitude towards the project. I pointed out that we had no experience whatever of strip mill operation or construction and therefore

could not be of any help in that direction. Nor had we the
financial resources to face up to a project of this magnitude...
It was clearly necessary, if the mill were built in Scotland, that
we would require to be associated in some way or another with
the project in order that friction could be avoided (quoted in
Payne 1979: 376).

There was at the time, in 1958, no current market demand in
Scotland for strip mill products and immediate losses would
be inevitable. But the government judged that the £4 to £5 million losses per annum would be less than the cost of unemployment benefit and other public assistance, and that such a
facility was a prerequisite for the development of motor production and light engineering in Scotland. Colvilles were thus
induced to undertake the venture and the Ravenscraig plant
was commissioned in 1963. It was financed by a £50 million
government loan, repayable over 20 years at market rates of
interest. Colvilles were obliged to raise £15 million through a
share issue but were still left with a massive debt in interest
payments. 'The mill, whatever its technical merits, had been a
financial disaster. For nearly a century Colvilles had kept
afloat, while others about them failed, by pursuing a conservative financial policy, by retaining as high a proportion of the
profits as the board could get away with, and by acting within
carefully calculated limits; the company had now been brought
to its knees by undertaking a project that it had thought
unwise' (Payne 1979: 405). There was insufficient demand for
the output of Ravenscraig in Scotland, despite the acquisition
of motor industry production for Linwood and Bathgate, and
when the industry was renationalised in 1967 Colvilles was
technically bankrupt, broken by the weight of debt.

The approaching exhaustion of some coalfields had stimulated investment in the mechanisation of potentially richer

fields in the 1920s, giving Scotland a temporary productivity advantage over other areas. In part, this was achieved by evasion of the 1930 Coal Mines Act which sought to curtail output. The Scottish mineowners managed to fix an unusually low minimum price enabling them to dump coal on English markets. This enabled them to resist rationalisation of productive capacity by keeping open small pits. But costs were kept up by the minimum wage agreement and poor market prices squeezed profit margins. Most Scottish mining firms sustained losses in the interwar years (Buxton 1970: 495). The reconstruction of the industry under nationalisation included efforts to develop the Scottish industry in Fife and the Lothians to compensate for over half the stock of Scottish collieries which were due to be closed between 1947 and 1965. Even without the unanticipated fall in demand, these projections seem optimistic and the performance of the Scottish division of the nationalised industry was very poor through much of the postwar period. In the 1960s Scotland was responsible for almost half the total deficit, and while this share fell as the industry contracted it continued to make substantial losses in Scotland (Payne 1985: 90). A regional price surcharge on Scottish coal introduced in 1962 to help reduce the deficit had the effect of deflecting demand away from coal. Physical conditions were much worse than anticipated in the new coalfields, and labour relations remained very poor. Rising costs and falling profitability in Scottish mining constituted 'a disastrous transformation' (Ashworth 1986: 233). Not surprisingly both output and employment continued to contract sharply.

Neither restructuring through merger nor state intervention in various guises arrested the decline of heavy industry. Nor were such transitional experiences confined to the steel-shipbuilding complex. Much of the residual manufacture of textiles in Scotland was reduced to a very small scale, although as late as 1930 Coats was the largest manufacturing employer in Scotland with 12,000 workers, producing a variety of kinds of thread. By the end of the 1950s that market had stagnated and this drew Coats into a series of mergers involving the remaining British textile manufacturers, absorbing Paton and Baldwins in 1960. The latter was the result of an earlier merger in 1920 between two woollen firms which were based in Alloa and Halifax. Coats Paton acquired a number of retail chains for woollens and clothing before being taken over in 1986 by Vantona Viyella (Payne 1992: 41). Like other textile combinations this corporation moved increasingly towards mercantile activities, importing textiles from the Far East.

Amalgamation appeared in the jute industry in the 1920s, following the end of the sandbag boom of the war years, but the industry was sustained between the wars by the demand from carpet and linoleum manufacturers. Like other industries, jute did quite well until the 1950s, falling victim to technological substitutes from paper bags to bulk handling and containerisation. Between the mid 1950s and the end of the 1980s the number of firms fell from 39 to 12 and the employment from 19,000 to less than 1,000 (Payne 1992: 42). Even linoleum collapsed within little more than a decade, overtaken by rising affluence and replaced by carpet. Little remains of the Scottish textile industry other than the quality knitwear manufacturers in the borders.

Much of this decline was part of the natural evolution of world industrialisation and the transfer of comparative advantage to new locations. Given the cramped conditions of Scottish shipyards, the ossified structure of craft based production, the declining resource base which sustained iron, steel and coal, it is unrealistic to expect these industries to have contin-

ued to prosper indefinitely. Given the advances in technology
it is even more unrealistic to expect them to sustain the levels
of employment which obtained at the beginning of the century.
Attempts to prop up these sectors seem, retrospectively, both
doomed and financially wasteful. But the decline in employment was not suffered only by declining sectors of the economy. Under the umbrella of subsidies and protection, initially
from the British government and since 1973 from the European
Community, agriculture has prospered since the 1940s. Mechanisation has reduced the need for labour. Tractors, combine
harvesters, hay and straw balers, better and larger storage
facilities all diminished the demand for labour. Between 1951
and 1991 employment in agriculture, forestry and fishing in
Scotland fell from almost 100,000 to 28,000. The real problem
posed by structural change was not how to protect employment in these sectors, which was either impossible or unwar-
ranted, but how to generate replacement occupations for those
displaced from their traditional types of work.

Decline and the Union

The pattern of development outlined above took place within
the Union and solutions to the problems which arose were
sought within that framework. There were two ways in which
change was managed, by sustaining demand and by seeking to
increase supply side efficiency. Wartime spending before and
during the two great wars provided a state-induced boost to
demand throughout the heavy industries, affecting shipbuilding, steel, engineering and coal. After 1945 nationalised industries were provided with markets by other state controlled
activities, so that the shipyards propped up steel and electricity generation sustained coal. Demand was thus boosted by

government spending and by the provision of subsidies in various forms. Similar aid could, of course, have been provided by an independent Scottish government. But with a low tax yield per capita relative to the United Kingdom it seems doubtful whether such a subsidy system could have been operated on as generous a scale as that which applied under United Kingdom auspices, especially in view of the fact that Scotland contained a relatively large share of heavy industry. It seems highly probable that an independent state would have struggled to hold the rate of decline, and thence the growth of unemployment, to that which was actually experienced by means of subsidised demand.

The second strand of the management of industrial decline was to improve the competitiveness of industry. This took the form of mergers and collusion initiated by industrialists themselves, plus intervention by the government, as in the attempts to rationalise shipbuilding capacity in the 1930s and in post-war efforts at restructuring. The new industrial groups which were created by mergers were not exclusively or even largely based or controlled in Scotland. It was, of course, the fear of industrial control passing out of Scottish hands which aroused so much anxiety between the wars. How might an independent government have handled the problem better? All accounts of Scottish, and English industrialists reflect a strong tradition of independence, so it seems unlikely that collusion would have been any easier or more successful had it been confined to Scottish firms, as evidenced by the mutual antipathies in the Scottish steel industry. Further some of the mergers depended essentially on a wider frame of reference, steel and shipbuilding combines bringing Scottish firms together with their counterparts in Ulster and northern England. Operation within a narrower compass would surely have increased the difficulty and diminished the chances of success. It is, of course, possible to argue that the policy of supporting declining industries was mistaken and that a much more rational strategy would have been to allow them to fail while devoting government subsidies to expansion. The price, of course, would have been the existence of even higher levels of unemployment. It does not seem very probable that a Scottish electorate would have provided a mandate for such a draconian strategy given the widespread antipathy to the Thatcher regime in the 1980s.

The causes and severity of structural decline were inherent in the organisational structures characterised by small scale production, labour intensity, and a limited resource base, all essential features of the Victorian heritage. There is no easy way to manage such a process of restructuring and the British record has been effectively criticised from both the right on grounds of wasteful subsidisation and from the left on grounds of failing to curb unemployment. Given the limited tax base and the strong representation of heavy industry in Scotland, it seems probable that the process of transition outside the Union would have been even more painful without the benefits of United Kingdom subsidies on demand and a larger framework within which to formulate new organisational structures.

Chapter 5

The economics of regeneration

The exploitation of natural resources: Oil

The extensive structural change which has affected all industrial economies in the twentieth century, usually involving the decline of established activities, has consequently imposed a need to develop new and replacement activities. In economic terminology, Scotland is a small and open economy being necessarily exposed to shifts in international production and trade. Success, in this context, depends on the possession or acquisition of some comparative advantage. In the nineteenth century coal and iron deposits, engineering skills and navigable river estuaries provided that advantage in the creation of the heavy industry complex just as changes in comparative advantage brought its decline in the latter half of the present century.

The possession of a scarce natural resource is an obvious source of comparative advantage and provided the most spectacular economic development in Scotland in recent decades in the form of the oil industry which was, like coal, iron ore and shale oil in earlier times, a fortuitous but finite natural resource endowment. Gas fields were discovered off the east coast of England in the 1960s, and oil in the northern North

Sea at the end of that decade. Oil production on a large scale
dates from the mid 1970s, the first oil coming ashore in 1975.
By 1980 the United Kingdom was self-sufficient in oil, and by
1983 was producing 50 per cent above its requirements. By the
end of 1991, over 1,400 million tons had been recovered from
the northern North Sea. Oil related sales comprised 6 per cent
of Scottish manufacturing gross output in 1989 (*Scottish Economic Bulletin* 45: 15, 79).

Oil and gas production is a highly capital intensive activity,
labour payments making up no more than 3 per cent of total
costs. But since proximity to the offshore fields is important
for many stages of preparatory and support work, Scotland,
especially in the Grampian and Highland regions, has
benefited from the employment impact of the industry. While
many of the mobile drilling rigs are not of British make, the
fixed production platforms are most advantageously manufactured within as small a towing distance from their final location as possible. Steel platforms were constructed at Nigg Bay,
Ardersier and Methil, while concrete platforms needing deeper
water, were built at Loch Kishorn and Hunterston in the west.
While the oil was piped ashore in Scotland, in the mid 1980s
it was estimated that only 16 per cent of North Sea oil was
refined in Scotland, at Grangemouth, and 40 per cent in the
United Kingdom as a whole, the bulk being exported in crude
form to the United States, Germany and the Netherlands
(Mackay 1984: 335).

The most obvious manifestation of the industry has been in
services supporting production, located along the east coast
and in Shetland and centred on Aberdeen. Around these bases
there has developed a substantial engineering and oil related
infrastructure. At its peak, in 1985, the oil industry employed
some 50,000 people in Grampian region and probably another

40,000 in the rest of Scotland (Pike 1993: 56). Revenues from the industry reached over £20,000 million in the mid 1980s. But like the natural resources exploited earlier, oil was sold on a volatile international market, the vulnerability of which was demonstrated in the middle of the decade as the price fell from $27 to $8 dollars per barrel in a few months as OPEC abandoned its quota system for production and deluged the market.

The collapse in the oil price severely reduced the revenues of companies operating in the North Sea. They responded by cutting exploration expenditure from £1,377 million to £737 million between 1985 and 1987 (Pike 1993: 63). Drilling was similarly curtailed, although the cost of keeping a rig 'moth-balled' could be £500,000 per annum, while a rig working half time could accumulate losses of four times that sum in a year. The downturn in the industry stimulated a move towards the development of satellite fields with lower development costs which adversely affected the construction and contracting branches of the industry. There were massive redundancies at all the major construction yards, especially at Loch Kishorn. On the other hand, high production costs meant that there was little reduction in output because of the high cost and techni-cal complexity involved in a temporary shutdown.

But the impact of the recession was impressive. Employment in North Sea oil fell by 14,000 or 15 per cent of the labour force over a period of eighteen months from mid 1985. Many small companies failed; they were the lower technology, labour intensive businesses which lacked the financial resources to ride out the depression. Many of these were Scot-tish owned. In Aberdeen the number of houses for sale dou-bled and prices fell. The industry readjusted. 'Rounds of mergers, asset swapping and general rationalisation swept the

industry. Where smaller Scottish companies simply disappeared, larger, international companies pooled resources,
negotiated takeovers or subsumed themselves within larger
entities' (Pike 1993: 67). By 1989 three main conglomerates
dominated the industry in the North Sea with 80 per cent of
the production and drilling services in Scotland, and 70 per
cent worldwide. All were American companies. By 1988 the
world price of oil had stabilised and drilling recovered in the
North Sea. Exploration resumed in response to a new set of
licensing awards. But the recession demonstrated the vulnerability of Scottish oil production to international market forces,
while the rationalisation within the industry in response to the
recession further curtailed Scottish involvement and thence
control over future developments.

The growth and fluctuations in the oil industry reflect several essential features of economic life for small open
economies. The comparative advantage given by the possession of a valuable natural resource confers substantial benefits.
By 1990 employment in companies wholly related to North Sea
oil exploitation in Scotland stood at 64,000 of which almost
52,000 was in Grampian region. There is no doubt that
Grampian's position enjoying one of the highest per capita
average income levels in the United Kingdom is a reflection of
the concentration of oil related activity. On the debit side, natural resources are finite and modern multinational industry is
not confined or committed to specific locations if alternatives
can be found. International price fluctuations determine the
scale of activity, together with the availability of resources and
the costs entailed in exploiting them. Oil exploration in Scotland is thus determined by forces which cannot be controlled,
except marginally, by government.

New industrial growth

The international characteristics of the oil industry represent developments which have been in process throughout industry for the past century in the trend towards the increasing integration of international markets and the evolution of multinational corporations whose activities extend over many countries and a diversity of products. In this context economic regeneration requires that such companies be attracted to establish their operations in Scotland. Major factors in attracting inward investment include the availability of suitable infrastructure, access to markets in the United Kingdom and European Community, available labour and capital incentives. The United Kingdom has been a major beneficiary from such investment flows, estimates for 1990 indicating a net outward flow of £21 billion and a net inward flow of £17.5 billion (Hill and Munday 1992: 536). Most of the inward investment has come from the United States, although recently both Japan and other European Community countries have become more important.

The establishment of new industries by foreign companies in Scotland is by no means new. Singer, an American company, established production in Glasgow in the 1860s, attracted by an established industrial and commercial structure, as well as the cheapness and docility of the workforce. When the Clydebank plant was completed in 1885 it was the largest sewing machine factory in the world with a capacity of 10,000 machines per week. Anxiety about the poor representation of such new industries in Scotland was voiced in the 1930s as unemployment persisted in heavy industry. The Scottish Development Council founded in 1931 was keen to attract new industries north of the border and this aim underlay the formation of Scottish Industrial Estates in 1937, while the commissioner for special areas advocated diversification of the industrial structure, as did the Clyde Valley Regional Plan published in 1946. By 1950 some 100,000 jobs existed in Scotland in factories built since 1937, and 80,000 of them were in the development areas (Saville 1985: 33). Some of this was a direct result of the war, such as the Rolls-Royce aero-engine plant at Hillington as was the fact that 30 firms had links with the aircraft industry by 1950. By that date a business machine industry had been established, as had production in radio and electronic equipment, and electrical engineering, as well as office furniture, and a small vehicle related sector. The attraction of new industry meant acceptance of branch plants with headquarters elsewhere, often abroad. While the bulk of businesses relocated in Scotland prior to 1950 came from the south and midlands of England, the number of jobs in foreign owned firms (mainly American or Canadian) was estimated at 40,000 (Saville 1985: 34).

Scotland shared the boom of the 1950s and 1960s together with the rest of the industrialised world, and achieved some diversification of its industrial structure into the consumer-oriented and science-based manufactures which were so scarce in the interwar years. Engineering, electronics, vehicles, food and drink and, later, the oil industry were part of this diversification. Some of this growth came from relocation within the United Kingdom as a response to government policy. The establishment of motor car production is the most familiar example, and was linked to the efforts to revive the Scottish steel industry by providing it with a market beyond the shipyards. But much of the expansion came in the form of multinational direct inward investment, so that by the early 1980s 80,000 Scots were employed in corporations owned overseas. In engineering these firms accounted for 40 per cent of all employment (Young 1984: 93–4). The bulk of this inward investment was American.

Electronics was one of the great successes of this structural transformation, with an increase in employment of 35,000 jobs between 1959 and 1983 (Firn and Roberts 1984: 298). By the latter date, this industry accounted for almost 10 per cent of employment in manufacturing. The origins of this industry in Scotland lay in the wartime base established in Edinburgh by Ferranti for the production of gunsights. By the 1980s, although the company remained based in England, the Scottish division was the largest in the company, and Ferranti was the largest firm in the Scottish electronics industry. But in 1993 the Scottish division went into receivership. In 1960 Scotland acquired an entry into the semiconductor branch of the industry when the Hughes Aircraft Corporation established a plant at Glenrothes. In the late 1960s Scotland gained other American electronics firms including National Semiconductor, Motorola, and General Instrument Microelectronics, and later NEC from Japan. The early growth was stimulated by low start-up costs, a common language, cheap labour and available skilled workers. Eventually 'Silicon Glen', which spread across central Scotland from Ayrshire to Dundee, encompassed one of the greatest concentrations of high technology industry outside the United States (Haug 1986: 109). The attraction of the location was reinforced by government aid and links with universities, such that Wang laboratories chose a location close to the University of Stirling in 1983, while Burr-Brown chose Livingston because it gave easy access to the Wolfson Microelectronic Institute at the University of Edinburgh. Heavy investment in the semiconductor industry established Scotland as the major producer in western Europe by the early 1980s

with 79 per cent of United Kingdom and 21 per cent of western European output of integrated circuits (Firn and Roberts
1984: 299). Foreign ownership was not the only element of
uncertainty in the industry. Most output was exported from
Scotland and many contracts were linked to the defence industry. This did not generate large numbers of jobs, 4,400 in 1985
out of 42,400 in Scottish electronics as a whole (Henderson
1989: 121). But it was the technological heart of the industry
and was thus crucial to the maintenance of electronics in Scotland. Even so the attractions for American firms reflect the
limitations of branch factory development. Wages were little
more than half their Californian equivalent even in the 1980s,
and lower than in many EC countries. The semiconductor
companies have managed to insulate themselves against pressure from organised labour by recruiting women rather than
men, by operating anti-union policies throughout the world,
and by locating mainly in the new towns to avoid the mili-
tancy of traditional employment centres. Motorola, based at
East Kilbride, isolated employees from less compliant influences by employing a workforce 60 per cent of whom lived
within three miles of the plant. While the branches of these
companies in Scotland have never been self-sustaining, it seems
unlikely that any country will be able to achieve such a status
given the internationalisation of industry. But there have been
spin-offs with some Scottish design companies being established, primarily in the Edinburgh area and linked to local universities.

Ownership and control

The necessity of attracting new industry from outside Scotland
together with the worldwide trend towards amalgamation into

conglomerates and multinational corporations has radically reduced the Scottish share of ownership in industries operating within Scotland. While, before 1914, much of Scottish industry was owned north of the border, the share has fallen markedly since the First World War. Initially this meant that ownership and control moved to England; more recently, as the process of internationalisation has accelerated, ownership has often passed further afield. By 1987 external ownership had reached a high level. The Times 1000 list of top companies, measured by turnover, showed that Scotland was the headquarters for only 5.2 per cent of the national total. In 1990 64 per cent of the top 200 firms in Scotland in terms of an index combining turnover and profit were Scottish owned, 18 per cent were owned in the rest of the United Kingdom and 11 per cent in the USA (Dow 1992: 622).

Loss of control has taken place steadily since 1918. The merger of railway companies into the government regulated groups like London, Midland and Scottish (LMS) and the London and North Eastern Railway (LNER) in the 1920s absorbed hitherto independent Scottish companies. The LMS took over the Caledonian Railway, the Callendar and Oban, the Lanarkshire and Ayrshire, the Highland Railway and the Glasgow and South Western, while the LNER swallowed the North British, the Forth Bridge and the Great North of Scotland companies. Bank mergers had the same effect. In 1918 Lloyds took over the National Bank. The British Linen Bank merged with Barclays in 1919, two years later the Midland Bank took over the Clydesdale and, in 1924, the North of Scotland Bank. The Norwich Union took over Scottish Imperial in 1913 and Commercial Union took over Edinburgh Life in 1918, while others like the North British and Mercantile moved their headquarters to London. In the chemical industry,

Nobel's and United Alkali were absorbed into ICI in the 1920s. Steel and shipbuilding experienced the same spate of merger and amalgamation resulting, for the moment, in the retention of some Scottish control. But the larger and stronger companies remained, like Standard Life, Scottish Amicable and Scottish Widows. By the interwar years the main economic network in Scotland lay in the financial sector, focused around the Bank of Scotland, investment trusts and insurance companies (Scott and Hughes 1980: 93).

The same trend towards concentration of control continued after the Second World War and throughout most branches of industry. In banking the merger of the National Bank and the Commercial Bank in 1959 reduced the number of Scottish banks to five. By the end of the next decade most Scottish banking was externally controlled, the Clydesdale being fully owned by the Midland, while the Bank of Scotland and the Royal Bank were under minority control of English banks. On the Clyde most yards were amalgamated into larger groupings, like Scott Lithgow, UCS and Govan Shipbuilders. Steel and shipbuilding passed eventually into public control, on several occasions in the case of the former. Both English and American ownership increased after 1950. Scottish Motor Traction became a subsidiary of Sears Holdings, and branch plants were established by well known names like Hoover and National Cash Registers (NCR). But the passing of control did not invariably move away from Scotland. The Royal Bank bought two English banks, Glyn Mills and William Deacons, while Coats merged with Paton and Baldwin in 1961 and retained control. By the mid 1950s the Bank of Scotland and Scottish Widows were at the heart of a network all the major partners of which were financial companies (Scott and Hughes 1980: 142). By the 1970s Scottish insurance companies had 12.5 per cent of total British life funds invested, including in Standard Life the fourth largest insurance company in Britain and in General Accident of Perth the third largest non-life company as well as half the main investment trusts. Standard Life and Scottish Widows provided the Edinburgh based centre while the Clydesdale Bank provided the main focus for Glasgow based interests.

Rationalisation was not, however, a guarantee of success for even the most apparently secure industry. In whisky manufacture, Distillers Company acquired ownership of over 50 other firms in the first quarter of the century including, in 1925, Buchanan Dewar and John Walker and Sons. This produced a company large enough to diversify production through investment in new technology which by 1939 included animal feed, pharmaceuticals, motor fuels, and a variety of chemicals. While the company remained based in Edinburgh, much of its new activity and investment was elsewhere, in Hull, Liverpool, Dagenham, Croydon and, further afield, in Canada and Australia (Weir 1989: 393).

Sustained export growth allowed expansion in the industry from 1945 until the late 1970s, as new distillieries were opened, at Invergordon, Girvan and Airdrie, while some which had closed between the wars, at Crieff, Rothes and Elgin, reopened. Productive capacity increased by 50 per cent in the 1970s alone. But the heavy reliance on the American export market was revealed by the massive drop in sales in the recession of the early 1980s caused by an adverse shift in the exchange rate and changing consumer preferences in the United States. Production fell sharply from 1978 to 1983 and then recovered modestly. Job losses were estimated at 30 per cent of the workforce between 1979 and 1984, and closure of several distilleries was a necessary adjustment. The growth of the 1970s had created an increase in external control, although about 60 per cent of the distilleries were controlled from outside Scotland by the early 1960s. The surge of acquisitions in the 1970s left only about 22 per cent of distilleries under Scottish control. This was further eroded in the mid 1980s and finally ended in 1993 (Love 1990: 103–4).

The effects of three different take-overs in the 1970s exhibited many similarities. One was an agreed take-over by a large British drinks firm, another was a hostile take-over by an American group, and the third was a take-over by a large European drinks company initiated by the shareholders of the acquired company who wished to realise their assets. Each company had 80 per cent of banking and insurance services removed from local control. Auditing, advertising services, banking and legal work for all three firms were moved to England. In addition the acquisition which was British based led to the transfer of substantial packaging, and transport services as well as the purchase of 30 per cent of its bottles to England. The latter represented a net loss of £500,000 to the Scottish glass industry.

The impact on the three companies was markedly different. The British company enjoyed a substantial increase in sales the impact of which exceeded the wider negative impact on Scotland resulting from the reduction of commercial links. The American take-over reduced sales and thus reinforced the negative impact of reduced links, while the European take-over produced a modest sales increase and a very small loss from broken linkages. Clearly the negative impact of such mergers is felt in the domestic service sector, while efficiency is usually improved and provides a boost to the economy through increased sales.

As a result of such restructuring, the extreme dependence of the Scottish economy on heavy industry was reduced. Buxton's estimates of location quotient concentrations for 1979 show much less diversity than those for 1929, indicating that the employment structure of Scotland was by the later date much closer to that of the United Kingdom, although there were still marked deficiencies in vehicles and miscellaneous manufacturing (Buxton 1985: 66). But one of the effects of this restructuring was to ensure that by the 1970s the great majority of Scottish industrial workers were employed by firms based in England or abroad.

Increasing reliance on multinational corporations controlled outside Scotland was almost certainly inevitable. Indeed, given its smallness, Scotland has fared well in that a number of major firms retain their headquarters in the country. But the mobility of modern multinationals means that plant can be lost as well as gained. By the 1950s changing technology was beginning to leave the conservative Singer company behind and its market share declined accordingly. The corporate response was a programme of diversification in the 1960s and 1970s which included some ill-judged developments, and led to an era of retrenchment at the end of that period. The consequences of all of this were felt in Clydebank, initially in a reduction in employment from a peak in 1960 of 16,000 workers. Some activities were relocated to lower cost centres abroad, but the problems also reflected the typical weaknesses of British industrialisation in poor labour relations, antiquated plant because of low investment, and poor organisational structures. By the late 1970s the factory was working at only one third capacity. A feasibility study for future development, financed by a grant from the Scottish Development Agency (SDA) and a levy on the workers, proposed a reduction in the range of machines produced, new investment and a wage structure which provided some incentive for the workers to improve productivity. The workforce was reluctant to accept the necessary redundancies included in the rescue package, and there was some disruption of production. But a further deterioration in world market conditions precipitated the closure of the plant in 1980 (Hood and Young 1984: 50–53).

There were other casualties. Massey-Ferguson transferred the production of combine harvesters from Kilmarnock to France in 1978 as part of a restructuring process, and the closure of the Monsanto plant in Ayrshire in 1979 was a response to an industry shift away from nylon to other synthetic materials. Since most overseas companies had located in Strathclyde, this region bore the brunt of the outward migration of the 1970s and the consequent loss of jobs. But other less prosperous parts of Scotland faced similar contractions. The Timex watch company established a plant in Dundee in 1946, attracted by cheap costs and skilled female workers. After two decades of success, labour problems and the attraction of cheaper labour in the Far East encouraged the firm to run down its Dundee operation in 1974. In the event only a small number of redundancies were announced, but over the next two decades employment was progressively reduced until the final acrimonious dispute and closure in 1993. There were even losses in electronics, Hewlett-Packard moving to Bristol in the early 1980s. The impact of such changes were not always to the detriment of Scotland. Hoover maintained its Cambuslang factory while closing down in West London, and NCR closed factories in continental Europe rather than Dundee. But within a multinational operation small plants, especially those with a poor productivity record and difficult labour relations, are exceptionally vulnerable, a point which appeared to escape some of the trade union leaders in the Timex dispute.

A recent study of the effects of external take-over on 25 Scottish manufacturing companies between 1965 and 1980 found mixed effects. On the positive side, many firms became better managed and better able to secure funding for investment and hence more competitive than hitherto. But many managerial functions were relocated away from Scotland, and professional services such as banking and accountancy were also purchased elsewhere (Ashcroft 1988: 136). There was a loss of autonomy and of crucial functions like marketing, and research and development. Such changes have affected the growth of business services like design, advertising and management consultancy which have become important intermediate services in recent years. But the firms surveyed benefited from improved management and greater access to finance making a definitive evaluation impossible. A similar analysis of 54 large manufacturing companies subject to take-over between 1965 and 1980, and consequently either losing their headquarters or main operation from Scotland, showed that profitability tended to fall, but sales performance improved and there was no effect on employment. The performance of the companies had not been adversely affected, but that of Scotland as a whole was disadvantaged by the reduction of linkages resulting from the take-over (Ashcroft and Love 1989: 213). Much of the activity in business services in the United Kingdom is now concentrated in the south east of England and especially in London, although Scotland has its own smaller concentrations in Edinburgh and Glasgow. But such firms are disadvantaged by the increasing external control of the Scottish economy since corporate headquarters customarily provide or commission such services. Scottish firms have also faced a problem in being required to provide a general range of services to compete in their local market but more specialist services to compete in the English market. One Glasgow consultancy has marketed itself as three separate concerns in England but as a single unit in the Scottish market (O'Farrell *et al.* 1992: 524–31).

The rapid structural change and deindustrialisation which has characterised recent decades in the United Kingdom has placed great importance on the creation of new small firms. Between 1976–87 some 20 per cent of the stock of manufacturing plants was lost with a disproportionate loss, by 50 per cent, in the larger units employing over 1,000 people. Nationally there was a severe reduction in manufacturing capacity. While all regions lost, the decline in Scotland was greater than in any other region of Britain, a fall of 30.8 per cent (Tomkins and Twomey 1990: 389–91). Within Scotland, Strathclyde did very poorly with a loss of 36.9 per cent, as did the small Borders region which lost 64.0 per cent. The same relative weakness in Scotland is shown by studies of new firm formations as is the equally disturbing fact that Scotland's relative performance appears to be deteriorating. An analysis of the period 1966–77 found that Scotland generated more new firm births than would have been the case had it had the same employment structure in manufacturing as the national average and if each sector had had the same formation rate as the industry nationally. But in the 1980s this relative performance fell below the expected level primarily because of the low rate of actual new firm formations (Storey and Johnson 1987: 162–6). Under the Conservative administration in the 1980s policy shifted towards the support of small firms, and the evidence suggests that firms in the prosperous south east were quickest to take advantage of such opportunities. Elsewhere, including Scotland, even with the stimulus of the oil industry, the response was much weaker.

West Lothian had a history of deindustrialisation through the 1970s and 1980s, culminating in the closure of the British Motor Corporation truck plant at Bathgate in 1986 with the loss of some 6,500 jobs which pushed the local level of unemployment to 21 per cent. It was, thus, a prime target for such innovation. A survey taken in 1989 found 166 new firms providing employment for 849 people. Most new firms were small, with one to five workers, and half of them sold 75 per cent of their goods and services locally. This suggests that they have redistributed income within the area rather than created new income via sales outside the region. Many of the firms surveyed had started with little capital, 40 per cent of their founders had no formal educational qualifications and 30 per cent of them had previously been unemployed. The undistinguished growth record of these companies and their high local orientation meant they made little serious impact on unemployment or the needed structural change. 'The new firms generally seem to be imitative rather than innovative in terms of their products and processes, and are not the dynamic forms of organisation that some have claimed. Most firms are very small, under-resourced and run by people with little business experience and modest aspirations. There does not seem to be much reason to believe that they will generate sustained growth in the future' (Turok and Richardson 1991: 82).

Why did Scotland generate such a poor firm fertility rate? One study of the rate of firm formation between 1950 and 1984 found statistically significant results for the thesis that the rate of new company formation was related to unemployment, both current and in previous periods. The results suggested that the rate of new company registrations was greater when unemployment was high but falling. The conclusion that such firms were created because individuals were 'pushed' into it is, of course, consistent with a pessimistic prognosis for their future (Hamilton 1986). A further study of businesses registered in Scotland between 1976–80 and those which failed between 1977–79 showed a link between high fertility and mortality, mainly in Grampian and the Highlands. But the worst record was found in Strathclyde, Central and Tayside all of which exhibited very low birth rates. These results confirm the findings of other studies in emphasising a congenial environment. Owner-occupied housing has often been identified as an important indicator both of economic independence and as a source of collateral for loans. In Scotland, with an unusually high level of public sector housing there was a negative correlation between new firm formation and the share of population living in owner-occupied accommodation (Beesley and Hamilton 1986: 283–6).

Recent examinations have identified Scotland's enduring weakness in new firm creation. A ranking of local authority areas in Britain by VAT registrations per thousand of working population for the period 1980–86 placed five of the ten Scottish regions in the lowest ten places. They were, in descending order, Central, Tayside, Lothian, Fife and Strathclyde, the final three rating better only than Tyne and Wear. Scotland had a lower proportion of population classed in social groups one and two, a smaller share of labour employed in small plants, and more external ownership than most other parts of the United Kingdom.

The final and major point, however, is that the firm formation rate is principally affected by certain dimensions of the economic and social structure of the region or county concerned. The case of Scotland provides a good example of this. Scotland performs poorly compared with much of the rest of Britain because it has low levels of wealth as proxied by home ownership, a socioeconomic structure which is under-represented in education and in managerial and professional skills, and a plant structure which to some extent militates against workers gaining experience of small firms' (Ashcroft *et al.* 1991: 404).

The service economy

In Scotland, like other advanced economies, the recent past has been dominated by the growth of the service sector, both in the creation of GDP and employment. The service sector contains a diversity of activities whose growth and decline reflect different economic and social stimuli. A variety of attempts have been made to systematically disaggregate services, a popular recent distinction being made between producer services, supporting manufacturing and productive processes, and consumer services provided for the individual. Examples of the former would include commercial transport, advertising and business services, together with research and development activities, while the latter would include education, medical services and retail distribution. Unfortunately such distinctions are seldom clear cut. Banks, for example, provide services both for commercial and individual customers. One estimate for Great Britain in 1981 divided service sector employment into 1.8 million producer services, 6.9 million consumer services, 2.7 million mixed and 1.5 million public services (Marshall 1988: 23–5).

While it is difficult to measure the precise links and causal patterns within the service sector, or between its constituent parts and the rest of the economy, several clearly defined strands can be identified. Some services do support manufacturing and primary production, most obviously transport and distribution, and also part of the financial sector. Such can properly be termed producer services. But part of these services, especially financial and professional services are 'productive' in their own right, for instance, in providing commercial advice. Their growth reflects the expansion of the productive process but also its increasing complexity and sophistication in, for instance, unravelling the legal obligations of a multinational corporation. Whether this represents the most worthwhile part of the service sector is debatable. But what is clear is that there is a very great concentration of such activities in the South East compared to other regions of the United Kingdom. One estimate based on 1981 data found that over 40 per cent of employment in producer services was based there, well above the regional share of total employment which meant that all other areas of the country were relatively deficient in such employment (Marshall 1988: 64). Consumer services most obviously reflect growing affluence, while the growth of the public sector services, other than in wartime, has often been explained in terms of the ratchet effect of the demands of voters and politicians' promises.

Taking a broad brush perspective, the service sectors including transport, distribution, financial services and professions can be regarded as substantially producer services, miscellaneous services can be regarded as consumer services and public administration and defence as the third type of service. One measure of their significance is employment generated per thousand people which reflects both growth over time and the regional variation. For Scotland as a whole this ratio increased from 146.9 per thousand in 1911 to 216.0 by 1971 and 266.4 in 1990 (Lee 1983: 32–3; *Scottish Economic Bulletin* 45: 63). But these figures were well below the British aggregate figure indicating a weaker representation of services in Scotland. In 1911 while Scotland was deficient in all services, the gap was largest in the case of miscellaneous, and consumer, services and almost certainly reflected the poorer incomes of a low wage economy. There were substantial variations within Scotland by which Strathclyde, Central and Fife did extremely poorly, and Tayside, Grampian and Highland not much better.

The underdevelopment of the service sector in Scotland at the beginning of the century, and in other industrial regions compared to the South East of England, is consistent with a low wage, manually skilled, industrial economy generating limited demand for higher income producer services and, in turn, a restricted demand for consumer services, as evidenced in the poverty of much Scottish housing. In the course of the present century the overall gap has narrowed, between Scotland and the United Kingdom, although a greater regional diversity within Scotland has become apparent, reflecting the partial success of structural adjustment. By 1971 the Lothians stood well above the national average in service employment provision, Highland, Tayside and Grampian were close to it, but Strathclyde, Central and Fife and the Borders were substantially below (Lee 1983: 33). In most respects the pattern was sustained through the following two decades. Even though the Scottish financial sector is relatively strong, with 20 per cent of United Kingdom life funds and 33 per cent of investment trust assets in the late 1980s, merchant banks lost accounts as a result of the take-over of Scottish companies and the relocation of their headquarters, while Scottish firms have exhibited a poor take-up rate for small business grants.

The main outline of structural change in twentieth century Scotland is quite clear, and is dominated by the decline of heavy labour- intensive manual industry. It has also been hampered by the loss of industrial control through mergers and the appearance of multinational branch plants. The emergence of new industries and services has been inhibited by the lack of an enterprise culture and, more potently, by the lack of consumer spending power. Estimates of per capita wealth show Scotland averaging 89.5 per cent of the United Kingdom level between 1980–86. A higher proportion of Scottish saving was concentrated in the lower wealth categories than the United Kingdom as a whole, and the asset composition favoured highly secure forms such as bank deposits, gilts, and listed securities. Mortgages in Scotland were only 57 per cent of the United Kingdom average, bank loans 86 per cent and bank and building society deposits 87 per cent. It appears that both business and households in Scotland have a highly defensive financial strategy as a response to a prolonged experience of economic vulnerability. 'This would be manifested in relatively weak consumption and investment expenditure, relative reluctance to borrow, preference for relatively high saving and a preference for holding that saving in relatively safe assets' (Dow 1992: 627–30).

Economic regeneration and the Union

The influence of government has clearly been important in the process of economic regeneration in recent decades because it has relied heavily on the attraction of employment from outside Scotland. The oil industry was, of course, the result of favourable geological conditions, but most modern manufacturing industries, like electronics, have a much wider choice of locations. Consequently the final decision about the establishment of a branch plant may be strongly influenced by the inducements offered by competing regions. As an open economy, Scotland has both gained from the inward migration of new companies and industries and lost by outward migration of both industries and people. Like any open economy, it is vulnerable to the relocation decisions of multinational corporations. Scotland has been relatively successful since 1945, having the advantage of available skilled labour, strong North American links and a distinctive identity. Whether an independent Scottish government could have provided greater inducements and attracted even more businesses is difficult to determine in even the broadest terms. But membership of the Union does not appear to have imposed serious obstacles to such regeneration.

Perhaps more contentious is the loss of ownership and control which has been progressing since the 1920s and which stimulated some of the earliest economic anxieties about the Union. This process has not been unique to Scotland nor has control passed exclusively to England. It has been part of a general expansion in the internationalisation of business. Some of this loss might have been prevented by a Scottish government. The railway mergers and the bank takeovers of the 1920s are obvious examples. But the balance of such change is hard to evaluate. Some companies which moved their headquarters south retained a virtually unchanged productive activity in Scotland, like United Biscuits, while other companies which have kept their headquarters in Scotland, like Salvesen, have few other operations in the country. In this Scotland has shared the experience of other geographically peripheral regions of the United Kingdom and western Europe, characterised by a heavy dependence on capital goods industries with high levels of market concentration and a weak record of competitiveness. The merger movement in industry, which has been so prominent a feature of twentieth-century development, has created large multi-plant operations with headquarters outside Scotland. Branch plant economies with a high level of external control are liable to suffer from closures, generate fewer white collar jobs, and produce lower levels of technological innovation than metropolitan economies. Recent research suggests that extensive external control does have a debilitating effect on regional economies and that it has been a major influence on economic performance (Harris 1989: 244). Small open economies, and Scotland is smaller than the United Kingdom and as open, cannot really dictate effectively to multinational corporations which have numerous alternative venues from which to select bases for their operations.

The impact of the Union on economic regenerative growth is less clear than it is with regard to efforts to arrest decline. Since it is always possible to do better, it can be argued that greater government assistance or energetic marketing could have brought in more work that was actually achieved. But the balance of gain between Union and independence was probably not very great in this respect. The economic record of Scotland in the twentieth century, while rather undistinguished, is neither different nor worse than that of most other regions of the United Kingdom. Furthermore, it must be recognised that additional incentives would have had to be financed from what would certainly have been the very stretched budget of an independent Scotland.

Structural change, especially when it involves the recreation of employment is an unfortunately slow process. But the intractability of the problem meant that the twentieth century became an era of growing government intervention such that economic success emerged as a yardstick for the performance of the political system. The importance of government was further reinforced by the fact that the nationalisation of much of heavy industry and the growth of the public sector meant that the state became the employer of many Scots in the course of the century. Economic performance, relative prosperity, and thus the economics of the Union have all become closely linked to the activity and performance of government to an extent far greater than could have been imagined before 1914.

Part III

Government and the economy

Chapter 6

Government expenditure and taxation

The growth of the state

The increasing involvement of government in managing the economy has been one of the most widespread and significant developments in the twentieth century. In the context of Scotland's relations with the rest of the United Kingdom the aims and effects of government policy have been both extremely influential and central to evaluation of the benefits and costs of the Union. Government intervention, in its most basic and immediate form, has comprised a substantial increase in expenditure by the state on behalf of its citizens which has been funded by taxation imposed on them. Beyond that, governments of all political persuasions have sought to manipulate the economy to achieve ends which include economic, social and political considerations such as the creation of wealth, and the control of inflation and unemployment.

The growth of public expenditure has been one of the major aspects of economic growth in the twentieth century. Spending by the United Kingdom government, at constant prices, increased from 14 per cent of national income in 1900 to 52 per cent in the Second World War (Veverka 1963: 114). Since then it has ranged between 36 and 48 per cent, rising to a peak in the early 1980s before being clawed back to under 40 per cent by the beginning of the present decade. In real terms, expenditure has doubled during the past thirty years to reach £203 billion by 1989–90. In order to finance such outlays, state revenue from taxation has increased substantially as a share of national income to fund the growth in expenditure (Sandford 1992: 27–8). This has generally matched expenditure, although some spending has been financed by government borrowing in wartime and in recent years such that the public sector borrowing requirement reached £36.5 billion in 1992–93, a sum equivalent to a little over 6 per cent of GDP, and to £50 billion or 8 per cent of national income by the end of 1993.

The scale of the public sector, and its apparently unstoppable growth, raises important economic issues because this expenditure is the manifestation of public choices made by the officers of the state on behalf of the electorate. This breaks the obvious and important link between individual choice and purchase characteristic of the acquisition of private goods. Numerous attempts have been made to formulate theories to explain the growth of the public sector. In the nineteenth century, it was suggested that increasing population, urbanisation and the complex economic systems required to allow modern societies to function necessitated government intervention. Some thought that as material needs were increasingly satisfied, citizens would transfer their preferences to services best provided by the state. Peacock and Wiseman (1967) proposed a displacement effect, primarily activated by the two great wars of the twentieth century, in which the unavoidable involvement of the state in controlling economic activity in wartime acted as a demonstration effect and established a new norm. Breton (1974) redefined this by arguing that the greater degree of coercion which has to be tolerated in war lowers the cost to voters of securing promises for the future from their governments. These ideas have also been linked to the notion that central government is best placed to generate a uniform quality of service. More recently the argument has been advanced that private and public goods are essentially complementary, such as, for instance, industrial advance and higher education, and this necessarily binds them together.

These arguments offer the positive case for the growth of the public sector; others have described the process in less favourable terms. Baumol's (1967) model of unbalanced growth proposes the hypothesis of a two sector economy, one of which is technologically progressive while the other is primarily not so. Wages in the progressive sector are linked to productivity but the growth which is thus generated increases demand for the output of both sectors and incomes within them. Wages in the backward sector will tend to follow those in the progressive sector so that costs and prices are increased in the backward sector without commensurate productivity gain. If the backward sector provides public goods, a choice will have to be made between reduced provision and increased taxation. Even so, the lower productivity in this sector will mean that it will attract labour away from the progressive sector, diminishing overall productivity. The growth of the public sector is, from this perspective, no more than an illusion wrought by the lower levels of productivity in that sector so that the growth of employment appears to signify an increase in provision. It also carries gloomy implications for economic growth by draining resources away from their most productive uses.

An alternative line of explanation depicts the growth of the public sector in a political democracy in terms of weak political control, or as the result of various kinds of illusion or irresponsible action. Buchanan and Tullock (1962) argued that while there may be general support to cut waste, no single group in the bargaining chain will have sufficient incentive to reduce its own opportunities to benefit since few voters gain directly from a reduction in government services. The voter will thus accept a growing tax burden providing he continues to secure benefits from it. But since voters like expenditure but not taxation, those seeking their votes can obtain the best of both worlds by increasing public borrowing. This allows the public to underestimate the relative price of public goods and future costs through fiscal illusion.

One of the universal features of public finance in recent years has been the growth of public debt to fund expenditure without commensurate increases in taxation. Some economists have been highly critical of such developments, bemoaned the decline of traditional prudence, and observed that such strategies are inherently self-defeating. Initially debt-financed expenditure will increase the rate of spending on current services and/or reduce tax rates. But in subsequent tax years or time periods difficulties will arise as new taxation will fund only the same level of public expenditure as it did previously while part of it must now be allocated to servicing the debt. This will require either further borrowing, or a tax increase, or a reduction in public services, thus disturbing the balance previously achieved. The point will eventually arrive when the actual provision of public services is less than was obtained before the debt-financing strategy was introduced, reflecting a general loss in welfare. But if political accommodation is reached in each period the debt will never be liquidated. Taxes will continually increase to finance debt service charges which will mount as new debt is incurred to finance some of the charges on the original debt, thus destroying the capital resources of the nation. In view of these conflicting interpretations with, in part, threatening implications, it is not surprising that the growth of the public sector has become a major focus for debate and controversy in recent years.

Public expenditure

The growth in public spending in the twentieth century has been marked by substantial changes in its composition. Central government spending grew faster than local government and reached a share of the total of 77 per cent in 1951, and this share has fallen only slowly since that date. While in wartime spending on defence increased in both relative and absolute terms, the most potent force in the increase in government spending in the longer run was the social services component which accounted for almost half the total by the 1960s. By 1990 the upward growth of social service expenditure had increased its share to 57 per cent, completely dwarfing all other types of outlay (Veverka 1963: 119; Sandford 1992: 30).

The growth of social service expenditure has been partly driven by demand through the increase in the numbers of those entitled to benefit, and partly from the commitments of political parties to help the disadvantaged in society. One influence has been the number of persons surviving well beyond working age and thus claiming retirement pensions. Another has been the increase in the number of single parent families, unemployment and the prevalence of part-time work for women which together drove up demand for supplementary benefit and income support. The effect of all such changes has been to generate a massive demand for social security payments in Scotland, as elsewhere in the United Kingdom, by almost 50 per cent in the 1980s alone (see above pp. 68–70). Spending under this heading increased from 22.3 to 33.3 per cent of total expenditure in Scotland between the late 1970s and 1989–90 while health spending rose from 16.3 to 21.7 per cent. Other forms of expenditure proved easier to curb, so that support given to industry and agriculture fell from 14.3 per cent to 5.8 per cent of the total. Gross expenditure in Scotland incurred as assistance to industry fell sharply from £242 million in 1986–87 to £129 million in 1991–92 principally from the near elimination of the regional development grant (*Scottish Economic Bulletin* 45: 82). The relative growth rates of some of the major elements of government expenditure show that those driven by demand via social welfare commitments grew much faster in recent decades than those which could be more easily restrained by political decision such as outlays on industry or housing (Figure 9). Even so, the disbursement per head of identifiable government expenditure in 1989–90 for the United Kingdom and for each of its four constituent countries showed that Scotland fared very well, averaging 21.8 per cent above the United Kingdom, 27.7 per cent above England and 14.1 per cent above Wales. In absolute terms this represented an expenditure of £531 per person in Scotland greater than in the United Kingdom, the main components of which were in education and science £134.1, health and personal social services £128.9, social security £74.1, roads and transport £35.6, housing £49, and trade, industry, energy and employment £32.5 (*Scottish Economic Bulletin* 19: 168). These differentially high public expenditure figures reflect the fact that United Kingdom spending is based on the principle of equalisation to compensate for social, economic or demographic deprivation. A shift towards derivation, under which system expenditure would be confined to the particular geographical area in which it was funded by taxation, would clearly disadvantage Scotland as well as other parts of the United Kingdom. Scottish claims upon North Sea oil revenues would open the door for similar counter-claims from other parts of the United Kingdom.

One of the reasons why Scotland has fared particularly well from the allocation of government expenditure in recent years lies in the formula-funding mechanism adopted in the 1970s by which the Scottish block grant automatically increases in relation to changes in expenditure in England and Wales in a fixed ratio of 10/5/85 (Scotland/Wales/England), known as the Barnett formula after the Chief Secretary to the Treasury at the time. This formula applies only to changes in expenditure, but this precludes Treasury attacks upon the specific level of expenditure in Scotland and has thus protected Scotland's relative advantage. It also provides flexibility since the Secretary of State for Scotland can reallocate spending away from the source which generated its increase (Heald 1990: 12).

Taxation

In response to the massive increase in government spending in the twentieth century there has been a comparable expansion in revenue from taxation. This has been marked by substantial changes in the importance of different sources of revenue. At the beginning of the twentieth century over half the total revenues acquired by central government came from Customs and Excise duties, most notably from the taxes levied on beer, spirits and tobacco which together generated 44.7 per cent of the total (Feinstein 1972: 73). Income tax accounted for 17.1 per cent and death duties a further 16.4 per cent of the revenue

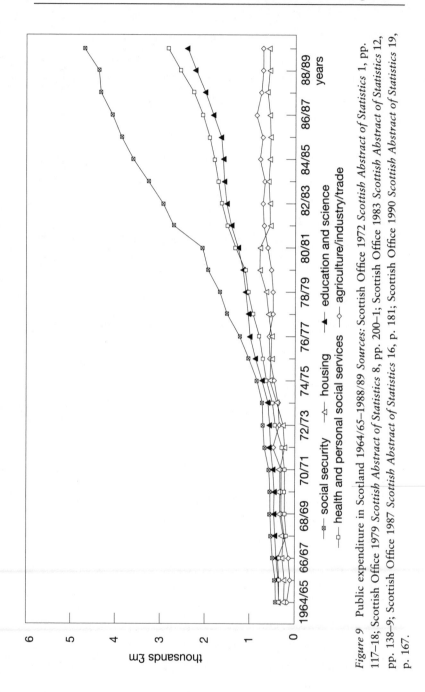

Figure 9 Public expenditure in Scotland 1964/65–1988/89 *Sources:* Scottish Office 1972 *Scottish Abstract of Statistics 1*, pp. 117–18; Scottish Office 1979 *Scottish Abstract of Statistics 8*, pp. 200–1; Scottish Office 1983 *Scottish Abstract of Statistics 12*, pp. 138–9; Scottish Office 1987 *Scottish Abstract of Statistics 16*, p. 181; Scottish Office 1990 *Scottish Abstract of Statistics 19*, p. 167.

in 1900. Even when the 1909 budget imposed supertax on incomes in excess of £5,000 per annum the maximum tax rate was still limited to 8 per cent (Kay and King 1992: 21).

At the beginning of the century, therefore, expenditure taxes provided most of the government revenue, from Customs and Excise but also from other taxes such as stamp duty, which was levied on legal and commercial documents. The land tax was levied on real estate, as was the inhabited house duty until its abolition in 1924, and the mineral rights duty, introduced in 1910 as an annual tax on the rental value of all rights to work mineral deposits. Other, and more recent taxes on expenditure include the motor vehicle licence duty and the television licence. Customs and Excise receipts were augmented by the adoption of value added tax (VAT) in 1973 to conform to the tax regime of the European Community. VAT is an expenditure tax which falls especially heavily on three commodities, namely tobacco, alcoholic drinks and petrol. By 1988–89 it accounted for 15.3 per cent of total tax revenue in the United Kingdom and had markedly increased in the twenty years since its introduction, as part of a general trend towards indirect taxation favoured by Conservative administrations and, apparently, less distressing or obvious to the electorate than increases in direct taxation.

The most impressive increase in twentieth-century revenue has come from income tax. In the early years of the twentieth century less than one million people paid income tax in the United Kingdom. Even by 1939 only four million income earners (20 per cent of the total) were liable to income tax. A couple with a joint income less than £225 was exempt while the annual average wage stood at £180 (Kay and King 1992: 21–2). Throughout the interwar period, basic income tax revenue was supplemented by surtax, levied on taxable incomes greater than £2,000 per annum, but only 105,000 persons came into this category in 1938–39. After the Second World War, the majority of workers were brought into the tax net and the growth of income tax revenue was the main source of increased government income in the 1950s and 1960s. Linked to income tax was the national insurance contribution which was started in 1948 specifically to fund retirement pensions, unemployment benefit and sickness benefit. Originally this was a flat rate contribution which bore most heavily on the poorest, but the growth of this hypothecated expenditure induced a change to a partly earnings-related contribution in 1961 and a wholly earnings-related tax in 1975. By 1988–89 national insurance contributions at 18.5 per cent of the total, and income tax at 24.6 per cent, were the two main components of total tax revenue.

The state has also taxed wealth as well as income. Death duties were first imposed in the form of estate duty in 1894, although it was preceded by legacy and succession duty on the transfer of wealth. Estate duty was an *ad valorem* tax on property being passed on the death of the owner and remained the principal such tax until it was replaced by the capital transfer tax in 1974. The estate duty had been easy to avoid, by the expedient of giving away property sufficiently long before actual death, and was almost regarded as a voluntary tax. Its successor applied both to lifetime transfers and to transfers at death. But the modest initial regime was subsequently watered down by raising thresholds and increasing exemptions until it, too, was replaced in 1986 by the inheritance tax which no longer taxed lifetime gifts and reverted, in effect, to the estate duty albeit in a less progressive form.

The newest form of state revenue is derived from taxation of industry. Until recent decades this was confined to the exigencies of war in excess profits tax. From 1937 until 1966 profits tax covered both distributed and undistributed profits. Company taxation, other than for war, dates from 1947. In effect undistributed profits were taxed at the standard rate while distributed profits were taxed as income tax according to the personal circumstances of the shareholder. In 1966 corporation tax was introduced. This falls into two parts, a tax on the profits and capital gains of the company and a tax on shareholders' dividends. Companies are taxed where they are resident.

A more specific set of taxes was devised to deal with the oil industry from the mid 1970s. Until 1982 royalty payments were levied every six months on sales at 12.5 per cent. In 1983 the royalty payment for fields licensed after April 1982 was abolished. The petroleum revenue tax was introduced in 1975 and applied on a field-by-field basis. Since then it has undergone many changes with generally increasing rates. The tax is levied on receipts less costs for location, extraction and bringing the oil ashore. In 1987 cross-field allowances and the right to offset research and development against tax were allowed. But some commentators have been highly critical of the government's record in this area.

> The Government has been spectacularly unsuccessful in achieving this objective (a stable environment) and the tax structure and rates have been subject to substantial modifications every year since they were introduced and have often changed several times in a year ... Worse than that, the interaction of the taxes is riddled with anomalies ... The combination of the height of the tax rates imposed, uncertainty about their future, and the random relationship of tax to profitability has now reduced the rate of exploration and development to low levels (Kay and King 1992: 184).

By the 1990s the Inland Revenue and Customs and Excise contributed the bulk of government revenue, and income tax took the greater part of the receipts of the former, changes which reflected an evolution as well as expansion of state income. Much of that increase in real and monetary terms came after 1945, although both world war periods had seen necessary expansion in government income and spending. Within the ambit of the Inland Revenue, growth in income tax was accompanied by taxation of industry from the late 1960s and the oil industry in particular from the later 1970s.

Expenditure and taxation: Scotland and the United Kingdom

The balance between tax paid and expenditure gained is obviously an important element in the economic relationship between Scotland and central government in Westminster, and has been the cause of debate and dispute. As regards the financial balance, it is clearly not possible to compute an exact net surplus or loss. Neither the income nor expenditure records permit this. As far as tax payment is concerned some categories are certainly determinate, such as income tax raised in Scotland (although not surtax which is only shown as a United Kingdom aggregate in the Inland Revenue returns), and death duties. Taxes on corporate bodies, however, may not give a clear indication of the source of their revenues, except in the extreme case of oil where much of the activity lies in Scotland. Expenditure taxes, in particular, can be misleading. Scottish producers paid a large share of the excise duty in the early years of the century, about 25 per cent of the United Kingdom total, because of the duty levied on 'Home Made Spirits'. In 1901, Scotland was the home for 156 of the 193 distilleries in the United Kingdom, the largest concentrations being found in the counties of Argyll (33), Banff (24), Moray (14), Aberdeen (10) and Inverness (10). But the heavy burden of the excise duty fell only formally on Scottish producers. They were able to pass the cost of the tax to their customers in higher prices, so that the effective tax was paid by the consumers of whisky some, but not all, of whom were in Scotland. There are similar limitations in official expenditure records which divide public spending, even for the recent past, into identified or non-identified categories for the four constituent countries of the United Kingdom. In 1989–90 the non-identified category of government expenditure comprised 21.8 per cent of the total for the United Kingdom, over half of which went to defence. This component comprised spending which applies indivisibly to the entire United Kingdom, like defence, overseas expenditures and some industrial expenditure (*Scottish Abstract of Statistics* 19: 169). The identifiable component is that part of government expenditure which can be identified from official records as having been made in a particular part of the United Kingdom.

As might be expected, information on the interwar period is rather slight, and must rely heavily on A. D. Campbell's pioneering work on Scottish national income. His estimates were based on incomplete data, but included payment of income tax and surtax, profits duties and estate duties and national insurance contributions. Under the heading of transfer payments, he included national insurance benefits, pensions, family allowance and postwar credits. As might be expected, the estimates for the benchmark depression years of 1924 and 1932 show Scotland making a net gain as transfer payments exceeded taxation, by £5 million in 1924 to increase the Scottish national income by a modest 1.2 per cent, and by £20 million in 1932 which increased national income by 6.2 per cent. By 1938 the rearmament-induced recovery brought Scottish transfer payments and taxes into balance, but by 1948, the final estimate in the series, Scotland had a substantial surplus of payments over receipts of £80 million reducing national income by 9.3 per cent (Campbell 1954: 58).

Inland Revenue receipts indicate the long-run pattern of United Kingdom and Scottish taxation payments. In per capita terms, Scotland has consistently paid less to the revenue than the United Kingdom average (Figure 10). Only in 1918 and 1919 did Scotland pay above that level, and was within 20 per cent of it between 1913 and 1922. The depression of the inter-war period was so severe that Scotland's per capita payments to the revenue were only 55 per cent of the national average between 1934 and 1938. For most of the 1920s and since the Second World War the Scottish figure was mainly in the 65–70 per cent range. After 1978 these data were not published sep-arately. There is little doubt that the low average payment made by Scotland reflected low wages and unemployment. The income tax receipts are not only the principal item of rev-enue but Scottish payments for this element of taxation remained steadily below the United Kingdom level. It seems highly probable that the same influences which restricted Scot-tish obligations to the Inland Revenue would also be effective in restricting payments through expenditure taxes like VAT.

The only explicit investigation of the balance of regional tax and expenditure is provided by Short's estimates for the period 1974–75 to 1977–78. These include motor vehicle duty, which was allocated on the basis of the number of licenced vehicles, and value added tax which was allocated on the basis of family expenditure patterns. Short's figures include the contri-bution of Customs and Excise, national insurance and local

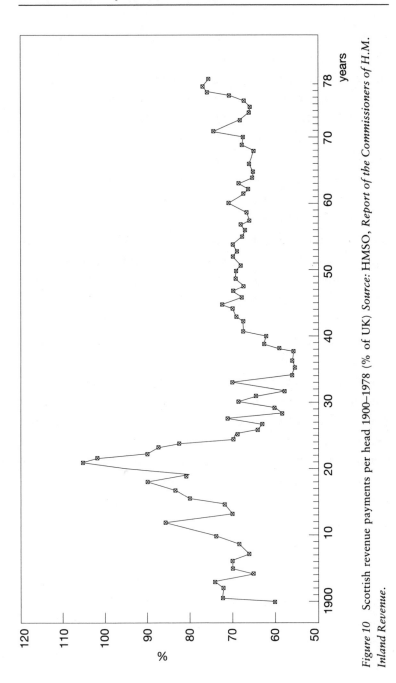

Figure 10 Scottish revenue payments per head 1900–1978 (% of UK) *Source:* HMSO, *Report of the Commissioners of H.M. Inland Revenue.*

rates to government revenue. The Inland Revenue estimates show Scotland making a rather larger per capita contribution, perhaps because of the inclusion of surtax and the allocation of petroleum revenue tax, but still shows a shortfall below the United Kingdom average by some 10 per cent (Short 1981: 72–5). The Scottish contribution to Customs and Excise was consistently close to the aggregate average, as were those of most other regions other than Northern Ireland, as was the case with rates. National insurance contributions were about 5 per cent below the average, and over the four year period the estimated Scottish contribution to the Exchequer averaged 94.5 per cent of the United Kingdom payment. These estimates thus confirm the long-run income tax data suggesting that Scotland consistently paid less to the revenue than the United Kingdom average throughout the twentieth century, as might be expected given low wages and persistent unemployment.

Heald's series for public expenditure per head for the four constituent countries of the United Kingdom, shows Scotland enjoying an average 20.5 per cent above the United Kingdom figure between 1973–74 and 1988–89, a share which increased over time to reach 23.3 per cent in the final year in the series (Heald 1990: Tables 5, 6). Throughout the 1980s, education and health took the largest share, together being worth 55.8 per cent of the total spending which fell within the discretion of the Secretary of State by 1990–91. Furthermore the effects of a shift in the burden of taxation from direct to indirect taxes, and the replacement of local rates by the community charge, reduced the redistributive impact of the tax system between regions. Even so, by 1988–89, compared to the United Kingdom per capita index, Scotland fared extremely well in all categories of expenditure with over twice the average on housing and agriculture, forestry and fishing, and over 30 per cent above the average in trade, industry, energy and employment, in roads and transport, in education and science, in other environmental services, and in the miscellaneous group. The lowest relative expenditure gain related to social security payments which still stood 6 per cent above the average. Overall Scotland fared worse than Northern Ireland but considerably better than either England or Wales.

The only detailed estimates for regional taxation payments and public expenditure gains for the United Kingdom are those made by Short (1981) for the four tax years from 1974–75 to 1977–78 which are summarised in Table 5. They show a substantial redistribution effect with six regions together sustaining an annual average loss of £3,308 million while five regions together secured a net gain of £2,347 million. Almost two thirds of the net loss was suffered by the South East of England, the rest was contributed by East Anglia, South West, West Midlands, East Midlands, and Yorkshire/Humberside. The North and North West regions of England, together with Wales, Scotland and Northern Ireland were the beneficiaries. In absolute terms, Scotland was the principal beneficiary with an average annual surplus of spending over taxation of £913 million, equivalent to about 9 per cent of Scottish GDP at the time. In per capita terms, Scotland was in second place behind Northern Ireland. A comparison of the expenditure per head between Scotland and the United Kingdom under the various spending categories revealed the main gains to have been made in agriculture, forestry and fishing and in trade, industry and employment. This doubtless reflects the impact of regional policy. The largest items of public expenditure were social security, health and education, although in the later 1970s per capita spending in Scotland was a little below the United Kingdom average. These figures also suggest that in the late 1970s

Scotland was paying tax at about 5 per cent below the national average. This is confirmed by more recent data for average personal incomes, disposable income, GDP and consumers' expenditure all of which tend to show Scotland's contribution falling between 5 and 10 per cent below the United Kingdom average in most years. Scotland also gained aggregate public spending at about 20 per cent above the United Kingdom average through the 1970s and 1980s, suggesting that for every four pounds paid in tax five pounds were recouped in expenditure.

> Given that this pattern is relatively stable over time, it seems implausible that Scotland, disregarding oil revenues, contributes more than the UK average in taxation. There is certainly a wide margin between this set of economic measures, all in the region of 95, and the public expenditure relatives at around 120 (identifiable public expenditure) and 130 (Scottish block proxy expenditure). Given these figures, it is clearly not in the interests of Scotland to pursue the idea of a precept for non-devolved services or, whilst remaining a part of the United Kingdom, to abandon the commitment to UK-wide equalisation (Heald 1990: 56).

Projections which suggest that Scotland's share of the United Kingdom population will decline to under 7.5 per cent by 2031 reinforce such a conclusion.

There seems little doubt that for most of the twentieth century Scotland has been a net beneficiary from the growth of the government sector and the redistributive effects of taxation and expenditure allocation. But such an interpretation has been attacked by nationalist sympathisers, asserting that it is the South East of England which fares especially well from government subsidies through the mortgage tax relief programme and from the concentration of Ministry of Defence spending in that region. Certainly a large part of the non-

Table 5 Estimates of regional taxation and public expenditure 1974/78

	A	B	C	D	E	F	G	H
South East	12236	725	14365	852	85.2	85.1	-2129	-127
East Anglia	1117	619	1243	689	89.9	89.8	-126	-70
South West	2626	618	2869	675	91.5	91.6	-243	-57
West Midlands	3229	626	3660	710	88.2	88.2	-431	-84
East Midlands	2322	622	2540	680	91.4	91.5	-218	-58
North West	4544	694	4464	682	101.8	101.8	80	12
Yorkshire/Humberside	3176	650	3337	683	95.2	95.2	-161	-33
North	2466	790	2112	676	116.8	116.9	354	114
Wales	2125	768	1791	648	118.7	118.5	334	120
Scotland	4507	866	3594	691	125.4	125.3	913	175
Northern Ireland	1500	974	834	542	179.9	179.7	666	432
United Kingdom	39848	708	40809	730	97.7	97.0	-961	-22

Figures are the average for the four tax years 1974/75 to 1977/78.

A: Public expenditure £m
B: Expenditure per head £
C: Taxation revenue £m
D: Taxation revenue per head £
E: Ratio col A/col C (per cent)
F: Ratio col B/col D (per cent)
G: Col A – col C (£m)
H: Col B – col D (£per head)
Source: Short 1981: 44–51, 64–71.

identified element of government spending relates to national defence, and many military suppliers and armed forces bases are to be found in that part of the United Kingdom. Spending in 1991 on defence was estimated at £453 per head in the South East compared to £274 in Scotland (Rosie 1992: 16). Subsidies to Network South East and the expenditure on the Channel Tunnel have also been identified in support of the claim that the South East is 'one of the most tax cosseted and feather-bedded economies in Britain' (Rosie 1992: 28). Such polemics are certainly stimulating, but the argument carefully ignores the taxation side of the equation. It seems highly probable the South East, even blessed with such advantages, remains a massive net contributor to the regional reallocation of resources by the government which has benefited Scotland and other parts of the United Kingdom on a substantial scale in recent decades. The recent reductions in mortgage tax relief were felt much harder in the South East than in most other regions and thus exacerbated that transfer loss. A 'fairer' allocation, or one more closely aligning spending to taxation would hurt many regions, including Scotland, far more than it would the South East.

A far more plausible line of attack against the notion that Scotland is a 'subsidy junkie', which was the stated aim of Rosie's television script and subsequent essay, lies in the attribution of revenues from North Sea oil. For the purpose of official statistics a region known as the Continental Shelf has been defined to include the profits and stock appreciation related to offshore oil and gas extraction. Incomes from employment generated by this activity are attributed to the region in which each employee lives. The Geneva Continental Shelf Convention of 1958 established the principle that the boundary between two states should be the median line between the line of the two coasts. As a result of this adjudication the United Kingdom secured 46.7 per cent of the North Sea basin. The Continental Shelf (Jurisdictional) Order of 1968 divided the United Kingdom sector along the parallel 55° 50' North into areas in which Scottish and English law apply, giving them respectively 62,500 and 32,800 square miles (MacKay and Mackay 1975: 21–4)

The substance of nationalist claims has been that the benefits of Scotland's oil should be retained in Scotland. Certainly if the GDP of the Continental Shelf region is added to that of Scotland, which obviously exaggerates Scotland's share, then between 1979 and 1989 Scottish GDP would have been on average about 50 per cent greater than it was. Since this notional acquisition would have been taken up entirely with the profits of operating companies, it cannot be assumed that all Scots would have been 50 per cent better off. A more realistic approach is to assume that the government revenues from oil, comprising the petroleum revenue tax, corporation tax and royalty payments, be accredited to Scotland. These revenues have varied substantially over the past two decades but were particularly substantial from 1981–82 to 1985–86 (Figure 11). The amount of identifiable public expenditure in Scotland is known. On the assumption that this was about 20 per cent above the United Kingdom average while taxation revenue fell about 5 per cent below it, the shortfall in taxation would be a little over 20 per cent of expenditure. This would imply that through the 1970s and 1980s public spending in Scotland was in deficit by about 8 per cent of GDP in the earlier decade and almost 9 per cent in the latter, within a range of 7–10 per cent. For an independent state this would imply a substantial public sector borrowing requirement, on the scale of the deficit which currently burdens the United Kingdom. If

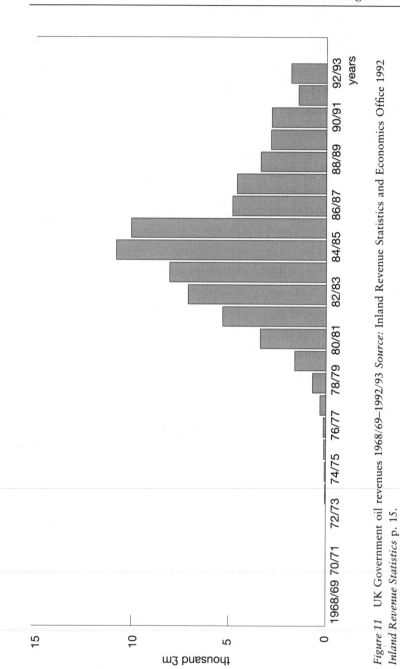

Figure 11 UK Government oil revenues 1968/69–1992/93 *Source:* Inland Revenue Statistics and Economics Office 1992 *Inland Revenue Statistics* p. 15.

Scotland is then credited with all the United Kingdom oil and gas revenues, certainly an exaggeration on what might be a negotiated allocation between independent states, the deficit remains virtually unchanged until the end of the 1970s, turning into a small surplus on national income in 1979–80. There follows a five year period, from 1981–82 to 1985–86 in which the oil revenues were at their height, in which Scotland, with the oil revenues, would have enjoyed a massive surplus at an average of almost 30 per cent of national income. But the fall in the revenues rapidly diminishes that notional surplus towards the end of the decade, and by 1989–90 the oil revenues would have been insufficient to cover the deficit. In that year, public expenditure in Scotland reached £15,079 million and exceeded taxation payments at £12,063 million by an amount equal to 8.4 per cent of GDP. If the oil revenues of £2,368 million are credited to Scotland for that year, the overall deficit is reduced to £648 million or 1.8 per cent of Scottish GDP. There are two inferences which can be made from these figures. Oil revenues do not offer a certain increased prosperity under an independent regime. The long-term imbalance between taxation and expenditure would require an independent government, possible hampered by an inherited 'fair-share' of the public sector debt of the erstwhile Union, which on the basis of population share might amount to £4 billion, either to cut services or impose large tax increases in order to cover that gap. Given the long-run average imbalance, without oil, this would imply either an overall tax increase of about 25 per cent or a cut in services of 20 per cent to achieve balance, or some combination of a smaller tax increase and expenditure reduction. Since Scotland has a limited number of high income earners to tax and many who fall below tax thresholds, together with a substantial proportion of its citizens who rely on social security and other state benefits, such choices would be painful in the extreme. In recent decades Scotland has obtained a very substantial, and legitimate, benefit from the practice followed in the United Kingdom by which taxation revenues are distributed according to equalisation principles in relation to need. A shift towards a system of derivation, whereby tax revenues would be spent in the areas in which they were raised, and which was implicit in the claim for oil revenues to be spent in Scotland, would have been especially disadvantageous for Scotland for most of the current century except during the five year oil boom in the early 1980s.

Chapter 7

Government policy: aims and mechanisms

The evolution of policy

The growth of public expenditure and taxation throughout the western world in the twentieth century has been accompanied by a growing expectation that a major function of government should be successful economic management. The incumbent administration is now expected to achieve a number of generally desired aims, including the maintenance of full employment, the control of inflation, and the generation of economic growth and prosperity. This increase in expectations, like public spending, was not planned but evolved from apparently innocuous origins. Some of these major strands of policy, particularly those seeking to confront the macroeconomic problems indicated above, necessarily are applied with equal force in all areas of a political system, so that United Kingdom policy to control inflation, for example, is applied equally throughout all its constituent regions. But such policies often have quite different effects in the various regions of the economy. The severely deflationary policies adopted in the early 1980s hit manufacturing employment far harder in industrial areas, like Scotland, Wales and the northern regions of England than they did the southern regions. Between 1979 and

1987 the six most northerly regions of Britain together sustained a loss of 1.37 million manufacturing jobs while the four southern regions lost about 700,000 such jobs. The fact that the former group was able to generate only a third of the service sector jobs created in the south meant they sustained a net employment loss of over one million jobs while the southern regions secured a net gain of 669,000 jobs (Martin 1989: 34). The important issue as to whether an independent Scottish government would or should adopt a different set of macroeconomic policies from those currently implemented by the government of the United Kingdom can lead to endless debate. Indeed, it may also be questioned whether, in the context of membership of the European Community and the increasing integration of policy at an international level, any small national economy can now exercise any real autonomy over such macroeconomic policy. In the context of a historical survey, it is not an important issue having had no historical manifestation for almost three centuries. But there are elements in national economic policy which have particularly impinged with a different impact on the various parts of the United Kingdom, and in this context regional policy and the closely related industrial policy have been the most significant.

An important early stimulus for the involvement of the state in seeking to modify the effects of the free market economy was the high level of unemployment experienced between the wars. Regional policy emerged from the recognition that high unemployment was not universal throughout the United Kingdom but was clustered in areas where heavy industry, which was currently depressed, was concentrated. In 1931 it was estimated that the unemployment rate ranged from 7.8 per cent in the South East of England to 19.2 per cent in the North region. Scotland, with an average unemployment rate of 16.1 per cent, shared the more unenviable end of the spectrum (Table 4). There were also substantial regional variations within Scotland. In early 1933, for example, unemployment stood at 70 per cent in Stornoway, 60 per cent in Wishaw and 54 per cent in Clydebank, although the rate in some English and Welsh districts was markedly higher (McCrone 1969: 91).

Initially the government reponse was a reaction to social deprivation designed to help labour to adjust to the changed work opportunities by providing training for relocation. But by the 1930s the unemployment situation was sufficiently severe to enforce a shift in policy towards encouraging the relocation of industry into the depressed parts of the country. From the mid 1930s until the late 1970s this formed the basis of regional policy. Given the long-term decline of heavy industry, which became apparent by the 1960s, state intervention was intended to revive local economies which suffered a major loss in employment by attracting new work in its place. The aim was, therefore, to reduce the inequality in unemployment levels and thence equalise the level of prosperity which existed in different parts of the United Kingdom. To a considerable extent, industrial policy especially when it concerned sectors nationalised after 1945, supported these aims. The decision to construct steelmaking plant at Ravenscraig to supply the motor industry established in the locality is an obvious and well-known example. The establishment of the North of Scotland Hydro Electric Board (Hydro) was intended to achieve social as well as economic ends, not simply to harness the power of the region but to prevent outward migration and regenerate the economy of the northern counties. Surplus production would be sold to the Central Electricity Board and the profits used 'for the economic development and social improvement of the North of Scotland district'. Indeed Lord

Airlie, later to become first chairman of the Hydro, argued in the early 1940s that the public sector would and should be obliged to provide a comprehensive and cheap system of electricity for the North of Scotland, since such provision could not be expected from the private sector. The Hydro, it was hoped, would improve the lot of crofters and fishermen, attract tourists and allow new developments such as forestry. The operators of the Hydro undertook a commitment to extend electricity supply throughout the Highland counties, even at the cost of a massive capital outlay (Payne 1988: 190).

Two decades later the Highlands and Islands Development Board (HIDB) was given a similar task by the government when it was established in 1965 in response to continued economic decline in the region. A programme for Highland development had been formulated as early as 1950 expressing the hope that growth might be achieved through agriculture and fishing, afforestation schemes, tourism and the hydroelectric schemes. In 1954 a Crofters' Commission was established to tackle the problem of land tenure. But the Highlands continued to fare poorly, and the expenditure of £220 million of public money in the 1950s failed to halt the outward migration. Some observers intepreted this as indicative of the inefficiency of government policy, while others thought that assistance to migration represented the only sensible policy for an area suffering hopeless decline (Simpson 1963; MacKay and Buxton 1965). The newly established HIDB endorsed the recommendation of the government's five year plan:

> First, a policy of concentration on objectives worth investing in, on the points identified as centres of the main labour catchment areas ... secondly, the development of forestry and forestry-based industries to give in the long-term a core of employment

in much of the region; thirdly, the complementary development of tourism both to assist consolidation in some of the main centres and give a supplementary income to the dispersed population engaged in primary and service industry.

The Board was given the wide ranging task of 'preparing, concerting, promoting, assisting and undertaking measures for the economic and social development of the Highlands and Islands' (HIDB 1965: 1). Twenty years later, the Scottish Affairs Committee reiterated support for the main objective of the Board. 'In our view it was Parliament's intention in 1965 that the newly created Board should endeavour not merely to retain the population base of the Highlands and Islands area taken as a whole but also to retain, as far as sensible and practicable, the existing settlement pattern; and we believe that this objective still commands general political support' (HIDB 1985: ix).

The period of intervention to counter the effects of the free market, in reviving depressed industrial areas and sustaining the rural periphery through the provision of jobs, housing and a range of welfare facilities petered out in the late 1970s as the Labour administration encountered financial difficulties and was eventually replaced by a radical Conservative government committed to free market solutions to economic and social problems. In effect, this returned policy to the type of emphasis which had prevailed in the 1920s, enabling individuals to adjust to market changes. But there was a more proactive aspect to policy in the 1980s through efforts to remove restrictions on the operation of market forces, together with a sustained effort to create a more competitive environment. This meant that regional policy declined in importance while industrial policy came to the forefront, and welfare provision was more narrowly targeted as a means of curbing the scale and influence of the public sector.

The structure of government: the Scottish Office

Within the context of a centralised state, it is not surprising that policy has been formulated very largely at Westminster in response to the aims of the government of the day. In many important areas of policy, Scotland has been treated as part of a larger national problem with policy conducted from White-hall. Regional policy, for example, was formulated and carried out by the Board of Trade. Similarly policy with regard to the nationalised industries, which concerned Scotland deeply, has also been determined nationally, although the influence of regional lobbies has often been influential, frequently to Scot-land's advantage. But the recognition of the separateness of Scotland was greatly facilitated by the existence of an admin-istrative infrastructure in the Scottish Office. This allowed the marked increase in the devolution of both policy co-ordination and decision making in economic affairs particularly since the 1950s. By 1992 the Scottish Office housed some 13,500 civil servants (Harvie 1994: 119).

The relationship between Scotland and central government in Westminster was conducted under a series of *ad hoc* boards until the establishment of the Scottish Office in 1885, although many boards continued to operate until 1939. The initial can-didates for inclusion under the remit of the Scottish Office, namely education and law, encountered strong resistance in Scotland against the transfer of control from Westminster, but without success. Education became the principal concern of the Scottish Office on its establishment in 1885 and responsi-bility for law and order was added two years later. There followed a steady accumulation of duties, including responsibility for agriculture in 1912, and for health, in practice mainly housing, after the First World War. But until the 1930s the Scottish Office remained located in London, while a variety of boards operated in Edinburgh. Eventually the Scottish Office opened an office in Edinburgh in 1935. Four years later the present structure was established, the Scottish Office finding a permanent home at St Andrews House in Edinburgh and absorbing the functions of most of the boards which were then abolished. The Scottish Office so constituted had four departments dealing respectively with agriculture, health, education and home affairs.

While the Scottish Office existed to deliver national government policies in Scotland, it was not always acquiescent in that task. As early as the 1930s it appears to have been more responsive to the severity and impact of Scottish economic problems than were Treasury officials in London. The main aim of policy was to enable the transfer of labour from unemployment blackspots to areas where there were better chances of finding work. But the scale of unemployment meant that this could only scratch the surface of the problem. A survey published by the Glasgow Chamber of Commerce in 1930 estimated that there would be 100,000 surplus male workers in the west of Scotland by 1934 (Campbell 1979: 170). Indeed virtually all scholarly investigations of interwar unemployment have concluded that the brevity of the period and the scale of unemployment was such that little could have been achieved by any form of intervention. But the Treasury remained resolutely opposed to funding private industry, restricting support to transfer schemes and some public works in housing and roads.

The Special Areas Commissioner for Scotland, appointed in

1934, pressed for industrial restructuring as the essential cure for unemployment. The Treasury response was that any viable project could currently find private investment, given the currently low interest rates, and that further involvement lay beyond the competence of government. As a result aid to industry was modest, reaching only 14.9 per cent of the total outlay in 1938 while social investment, particularly sewage schemes, took pride of place. Differences between the Scottish Office and the Treasury were exacerbated in the late 1930s by the attempts of the latter to reschedule special areas on the basis of unemployment rates according to increasingly stringent tests. The criterion of a 25 per cent level of unemployment was augmented by a requirement that 40 per cent of all insured population should be engaged in a single or closely related industry. This together with an additional test relating to the proportions of men and women who had been unemployed for a year would have eliminated from the assistance programme most of the 28 areas in Scotland which had qualified under the original criteria. The Scottish Office stressed the need for a programme of industrial diversification, a necessity temporarily concealed by the revival of the heavy industries through rearmament demand in sharp contrast to the 'more conventional, and less concerned, wisdom of Whitehall, which questioned the desirability of the policy for the Special Areas even in the mid 1930s, and which continued to regard policy as a short-run expedient' (Campbell 1979: 182).

The formal acquisition of economic functions by the Scottish Office dates from the establishment of the Scottish Economic Planning Board in 1964. This comprised officials from a variety of civil service departments in Westminster, under the aegis of the Scottish Office, charged with the task of co-ordinating the policies of those departments in Scotland. It was superseded in 1973 by the Scottish Economic Planning Department (SEPD) which was created as a result of the appointment of a Minister of State at the Scottish Office to co-ordinate North Sea oil development. The SEPD took over regional and industrial policy in Scotland, and oversight of the Scottish Development Agency (SDA) which was set up in 1975. The SEPD became the Industry Department for Scotland in 1983, reflecting the current ideology, with responsibility for regional and industrial policy, and a variety of economic agencies including the five new town corporations, the HIDB, and the two Scottish electricity boards.

The growth of the functions of the Scottish Office was accompanied by increased financial powers. From the late nineteenth century until the Second World War, the allocation of resources to Scotland was determined according to the 'Goschen formula' devised in 1885 and named after the current Chancellor of the Exchequer. According to this formula, the budget for expenditure in Scotland was based on the probate duty raised in 1885, of which Scotland provided 11 per cent of the United Kingdom total (Midwinter *et al.* 1991: 100). It was also close to Scotland's share of United Kingdom population. This formula proved beneficial for Scotland as the expenditure rate remained unchanged although Scotland's share of the United Kingdom population declined in the following half century. After 1945 this system was replaced by a process of bargaining between the Scottish Office and the Treasury. This also proved advantageous for Scotland through a combination of special pleading on the grounds of specific need, and because the small scale of the requisite budget appeared modest by United Kingdom standards. In 1978 the funding process reverted to the block grant system, the expenditure being in the control of the Secretary of State, intended as part of a devolutionary restructuring by the Labour administration. This set the 10/85/5 ratio of expenditure grant between Scotland, England and Wales which has been retained ever since. By the end of the 1970s the role of the Secretary of State in economic affairs had been substantially augmented.

Local government

During the course of the twentieth century the volume and cost of services provided by local authorities have increased greatly, including housing, transport, law and order, education and health. Many of these have been demand driven by rising expectations as well as by additional consumers, and by the fact that the link between consumption and payment has not been direct. This has been partly because ratepayers do not pay for services such as schools directly, but indirectly as part of a general tax. Furthermore, some citizens have not been ratepayers, and also the share of the total cost borne by central government through grants has grown sharply. In 1881–82 only 6 per cent of the expenditure of Scottish local authorities was funded by central government grants. By 1947–48 this share had risen to 33 per cent (Baird 1954: 181). By 1988–89 a much increased local authority expenditure was still dominated by education and housing, respectively accounting for £1,977 million and £1,325 million in a total revenue expenditure of £6,198 million. By then, government grants accounted for 47.5 per cent of revenue income (*Scottish Abstract of Statistics* 19: 169–70).

Since the mid 1970s the combined effects of escalating public expenditure, public sector deficits and shifting political preferences has imposed an ever increasing pressure to constrain local authority spending. Pressure was imposed on the Scottish

Office by the introduction of a convention by the Treasury that the total expenditure of Scottish local authorities would be regarded as part of the Scottish spending total as defined in the Public Expenditure Survey, with the implicit threat that excessive spending would be recouped in other ways. In 1977 the central grant was limited so that councils had to make compensatory cuts in services if expenditure exceeded prediction. Later grants were withdrawn in cases where local government spending exceeded the predetermined level. The share of local authority spending funded by the grant fell in the late 1970s by 7.5 per cent. Additional powers were assumed in legislation in 1981 and 1982 allowing the Secretary of State to reduce the grant of any council and compel it to cut its rate poundage where planned expenditure was deemed by the Scottish Office to be unreasonable. The 1980s saw a variety of local authority responses to central government attempts to restrict spending and protect ratepayers. Short-term strategies prevailed with creative accounting, increased charges, and tax increases being adopted. Council house rents, in particular, increased markedly although from a very low base resulting from decades of subsidy. Another attempt to increase visible accountability was the introduction of the community charge as a replacement for rates, under the assumption that a flat rate charge was a 'fair' levy for services which were equally available to all citizens.

Since the 1960s central government has consistently sought to control local expenditure. The revenue support grant, and its predecessor the rate support grant, determines the overall level of local expenditure on which the grant will be based, and also declares the share of expenditure which it will fund. This provides two means of curtailing expenditure, or at least forcing local authorities to 'act responsibly' by passing the costs on to their constituents. The grant award for 1989–90 provided estimates of what the community charge should be, another attempt to force councils to act with fiscal responsibility (or make them take the blame for an unpopular tax). The subsequent replacement of the poll tax by a series of banded changes represented a further round in the continuing conflict between local and central government in Scotland, opinion polarised both by constituencies and political allegiances.

Agencies of the state

During the period since 1945, there have emerged a number of agencies in Scotland, operating under the authority of the Scottish Office, through which policy has been channelled. They have provided a means by which the Scottish Office has influenced the actions of local authorities and sought to implement central government policy. The origins of such agencies extend back to the First World War when the first Scottish National Housing Company was established to provide housing at Rosyth for dockyard workers. A second company was formed in 1926 and funded by the Public Works Loan Board and the Scottish Board of Health to provide houses throughout Scotland using steel to provide both demand for a depressed industry and alleviation for the housing shortage (Begg 1987: 47, 53–5). In 1937 the Commissioner for Special Areas was appointed chairman of the newly founded Scottish Special Housing Association (SSHA). But the organisation soon secured permission to build outside the special areas and fell more directly under the control of the Scottish Office, a position which was confirmed by the allocation of construction contracts for wartime military and industrial personnel and subsequently for other agencies like those engaged in forestry and electricity generation.

As a major Scottish problem, responsibility for which fell primarily upon local government, housing provision was an area in which Scottish Office intervention through various agencies became increasingly important after 1945. Some local authorities were opposed to the solutions envisaged by central government. During the Second World War, the Secretary of State for Scotland established the Clyde Valley Planning Committee, bringing together 18 local authorities to commission, with a grant from the Scottish Office, the Clyde Valley Regional Plan. It was published in 1946 and became the blueprint for the regeneration of the region. The dominant theme of the plan identified a strategy to deal with the dreadful housing conditions and overcrowding characteristic of the region. It proposed the establishment of a green belt around Glasgow to prevent the city merging with the surrounding towns, and the establishment of four new towns at East Kilbride, Cumbernauld, Bishopton and Houston in order to relieve the pressure of population on housing in Glasgow by dispersing some of the people. This solution did not secure the approval of Glasgow Corporation which vigorously opposed the strategy in general and the establishment of new towns in particular.

The New Towns Act of 1946 allowed the Secretary of State to designate new towns to be built and run by government-appointed development corporations which would borrow funds from the Exchequer and repay the debt from rents and other revenues. Development corporations had the power to buy land by compulsory purchase, to undertake housing projects and to provide a wide range of services, subject to ministerial veto. The senior members of the corporation were also, of course, appointed by the Scottish Office. The official view was that new towns would be more amenable to taking Glasgow overspill population than existing local authorities and the designation of East Kilbride in 1947 provided central government with an appropriate means by which to implement its policy. So successful was the strategy that during the 1950s the population target for East Kilbride was revised upwards by the Scottish Office. The success of the venture was greatly helped by the transfer of the Mechanical Engineering Research Laboratory from Teddington to East Kilbride, for which the Scottish Office lobbied strenuously against opposition from Stevenage in Hertfordshire. It was confirmed by the establishment of Rolls-Royce in the town in the 1950s, a relocation which was secured by the award of government aircraft contracts. In the following decade the Inland Revenue was also prevailed upon to relocate in East Kilbride (Smith 1979: 77).

By the early 1950s Glasgow Corporation recognised the inescapability of the overspill policy, and accepted the Scottish Office decision to designate a second new town in the area at Cumbernauld in 1956. But there was considerable dispute about which bodies should meet the costs of the overspill programme. Eventually Glasgow did agree to contribute towards the cost of redistributing its citizens, and in 1959 signed an agreement with East Kilbride, Cumbernauld and Glenrothes to pay £14 per head for ten years for every family relocated to the new towns. By 1964 Glasgow Corporation had signed 57 such overspill agreements with local authorities from Wick to Dumfries. But so successful was East Kilbride in attracting Glaswegians that it was agreed that, in this particular case, Glasgow would only pay for those families whose principal bread winner was not employed in East Kilbride (Smith and Farmer 1985: 54–6).

The SSHA constituted another agency through which Scottish Office policy could be implemented, although the involvement of the SSHA in building and renting housing met with opposition from established local authorities. During the Labour administration after 1945 the SSHA was marginalised and, in particular, it was kept out of Glasgow. Consequently its building programme was restricted to smaller towns like Kilmarnock and Clydebank, and to providing housing for the National Coal Board which opened new pits throughout central Scotland (Rodger and Al-Qaddo 1989: 195). But the SSHA enjoyed a resurgence in the 1950s under a Conservative administration, and became a contributor to the overspill housing programme once the conflict between the Scottish Office and Glasgow Corporation had finally been resolved. The city authority undertook the renewal of the inner city areas, and the development corporations of the new towns were empowered, with Treasury loans, to build houses with, after 1957, SSHA assistance.

> If the joint overspill initiative – SSHA and Glasgow Corporation – literally cemented better practical relations between the two authorities, it nevertheless represented an attempt by the Scottish Office, through the SSHA, to intervene in the heartland of Scottish labour in housing politics by reducing the size and influence of Glasgow, by boosting the power of adjacent burghs, and by obtaining a say in the redevelopment programme (Rodger and Al-Qaddo 1989: 199).

Many SSHA programmes were built outside the main local authorities to provide housing which was critical to secure inward investment, as at Linwood, for the forestry and paper manufacture around Fort William, and along the Moray Firth and in the Shetlands when oil production began. It was also one of the many agencies involved in the Glasgow Eastern Area Renewal (GEAR) project in the 1970s.

The SSHA operated largely at the behest of the Scottish Office, which provided contracts and funding, although it also acted as a barrier between central government and local authorities. SSHA initiatives needed the support of the Scottish Office to reach fruition, but the latter would have faced more direct opposition and probably intransigence in its attempts to influence local authorities without the intermediate involvement of the association. As the second largest supplier of rented accommodation in Scotland, over 110,000 houses during its fifty year history, the SSHA was able to act as Scottish Office agent in taking a leading role in raising rents in the late 1950s, which were exceptionally low, for political reasons, in many Labour controlled authorities. Similarly housing provision outside the major authorities, supported by the new towns, undermined the political grip of major local authorities and paved the way for the reconstruction of local government in the 1970s. But eventually the SSHA itself fell victim to political change, being abolished in 1989 and replaced by Scottish Homes and a further shift towards a private and decentralised housing market.

The new town programme was initially stimulated by the housing overspill problem. But to succeed it needed to be accompanied by economic regeneration and this aim was pursued through the provision of industrial estates. The financial aid provided under the Special Areas Act was extended to support Scottish Industrial Estates Ltd, incorporated in 1937, together with three other special areas in England and Wales. These estates were intended to attract light industry into areas with relatively high levels of unemployment. Four were established in Scotland by the outbreak of war at Hillington, Carfin, Chapelhall and Larkhall. In the decade after 1945 the number of estates increased, mainly in what became the Strathclyde region, but also included Dundee and Inverness (Trotman-Dickenson 1961: 46). The five designated new towns gradually became regarded as growth points, and Irvine, the last to be designated in 1966, was intended as such from the outset.

> Irvine had already become in effect a growth area and the Scottish Office was anxious to stimulate more intensive industrial expansion. This was to be done by providing the town with industrial estates, a wide variety of factory premises for sale or to rent, and a readily available supply of good housing for incoming workers, set within a high quality urban environment. The Scottish Office concluded that the best way of realising these ambitions was to designate Irvine as a new town and thereby ensure that most of the infrastructure would be established by a development corporation. The implication was that such a body could handle this task more effectively than a local authority, even with support from the Scottish Special Housing Association and Scottish Industrial Estates Corporation (Smith and Farmer 1985: 59).

The success of the overspill policy was indicated in the projection made by Strathclyde Regional Council that Glasgow would have surplus municipal housing by the 1980s, and this persuaded the Scottish Office to terminate the plan for a fifth new town at Stonehouse, effectively to be an offshoot of East Kilbride, in 1976. Instead support was given to the development of eastern Glasgow and the senior staff working on the Stonehouse project were transferred to GEAR.

The nationalised industries controlled in Scotland, like the electricity boards, constituted another vehicle for public policy. Under electricity nationalisation in 1948 the North of Scotland Hydro was the only board to retain its independence with the right to sell bulk supplies. In 1951 the control of Scottish electricity production was ceded to the Scottish Office, and the Hydro became an important agency for the, heavily subsidised, economic regeneration of the Highlands. By 1960, 400 roads had been built or reconstructed by the Board and one quarter of them handed over to local authorities free of charge. A large number of new rural consumers were linked to the distribution network 'although the Board's income from sales of electricity to many of these newly connected consumers would barely cover the interest charges on the distribution capital investment, far less the cost of electrical generation and transmission' (Payne 1988: 202). By the mid 1960s, 95 per cent of farms in the Board's area were supplied and by the early 1970s so were 90 per cent of crofts. In total, by the early 1960s over 210,000 new consumers were connected, with sales of electricity growing at 12.5 per cent per annum through the 1950s. While there was some increase in industrial consumers, the share was low compared to the United Kingdom as a whole. 'By the end of the 1960s, over a quarter of the Board's consumers were being supplied on an uneconomic basis, and the estimated annual loss in providing and maintaining services to them was £1.75 million' (Payne 1988: 208). Costs were kept higher than they might have been by the refusal of the Board either to raise tariffs or apply differential tariffs so that consumers in eastern coastal areas subsidised those in the rural west. But the social objectives were never fully realised. The Highland economy was not transformed, outward migration did not cease, unemployment remained high, and new industry was not attracted on any substantial scale. But the policy of the Board was understandably popular in the region, so that when proposals were formulated to merge with the South of Scotland Electricity Board (SSEB) there was a massive public protest in the Hydro area and considerable wrangling between the two producers. The SSEB complained that it made substantial losses in importing electricity from the north compared to the profits it could achieve by increasing its own capacity, a charge which was strongly rejected. In the event, the widespread opposition and the imminence of a general election led the government to reject the proposed amalgamation.

The failure to secure regeneration of the Highlands through the agency of the Hydro Electric Board paved the way for another statutory agency, the Highlands and Islands Development Board. This agency was given considerable powers to

> give financial assistance by way of grant, or loan, or ... equity subscription, towards the capital cost of new or developing enterprises; it can set up and carry on, either directly or through an agent, any business or undertaking; it can undertake research and promotion, provide advisory, management and training services, acquire land, erect factories, and provide equipment and services; and it can, and often does, make representations to the Government on matters of concern to the Highlands and Islands generally (HIDB 1985: vi).

But the HIDB also revealed the limitations of such agencies. Its flexibility and independence raised expectations, and it soon became subject to pressure from interests which had very different visions of the Highlands including those who wanted to preserve a way of life 'which seems to mean crofters of an idealised character exempt from the ordinary laws of making a real livelihood' to those who wanted to destroy the crofting life as 'false, uneconomic and rotted by subsidies' in favour of manufacturing or tourism. There was also some confusion caused by the overlap between the functions of the Board and local authorities and other agencies, like the Scottish Tourist Board, and the fact that revival of employment opportunities in the Highlands on a substantial scale had to wait until the

1970s and the advent of the oil industry.

Scottish development: agency and enterprise

Much of the explicit economic involvement of the government
in Scotland in the last two decades has come through the Scottish Development Agency (SDA), which was established in
1975 and its successor Scottish Enterprise which came into
operation in 1991. The initial guidelines for the agency
identified four tasks, namely to further economic development,
maintain and safeguard employment, promote efficiency and
competitiveness, and improve the environment. It was funded
mainly by grant-in-aid through the public expenditure programmes of the SEPD, and its remit included investment in
industry through loans or equity, taking over responsibility for
the provision of publicly owned factories from the Scottish
Industrial Estates Corporation, and the clearance of derelict
land. These functions were extended to include urban renewal
and the co-ordination of the GEAR project. But the agency
was denied power to give financial assistance to industry under
the 1972 Industry Act, although these were crucial powers held
by similar agencies in other countries like the Republic of Ireland. From 1977 onwards the SDA took over the co-ordination of all efforts to attract foreign investment to Scotland
which had hitherto been shared by various bodies such as the
new town development corporations, regional and district
councils, and the HIDB. In 1979 the agency took over the long
established work of the Scottish Council (Development and
Industry) in attracting overseas firms to Scotland, additional
government funding reflecting increasing international competition, especially successful in the case of the Irish.

In the later 1970s much of the agency's work was concerned

with industrial estates and land renewal. But the change of government in 1979 brought a reorientation of its goals, emphasising the attraction of inward investment and industrial promotion, while the requirement to sustain employment was dropped and the funding aspect of its remit shifted from providing finance to facilitating the acquisition of funds from commercial sources. The Locate in Scotland (LIS) office set up in the early 1980s brought together the agency and the SEPD providing, for the first time, an integrated organisation for the attraction of inward investment, with offices in Scotland and overseas, which could co-ordinate a relocation exercise through all its stages. This initiative achieved a sharp increase in relocations and inward investment. Further changes in the attitude of government to state involvement heralded the closure of the agency, which was announced in 1988.

The SDA was superseded by Scottish Enterprise in 1991. On its inception the new agency absorbed three existing bodies, the Scottish Industrial Estates Corporation with its 145 industrial estates, the Small Industries Council for Rural Areas in Scotland with its portfolio of loans, and the department of the Scottish Office which was responsible for providing grants for land reclamation to local authorities. It also acquired three new functions, the provision of investment to industry, the industrial promotion of Scotland overseas to attract inward investment, and the co-ordination of urban redevelopment schemes such as GEAR (Hood 1991: 4).

A new set of agencies were devised in the form of Local Enterprise Companies (LEC) which were directed by the private sector, and inherited the functions of the disbanded SDA and HIDB. There are 22 LECs in Scotland, nine in the HIDB area, co-ordinated by Highlands and Islands Enterprise while the remainder fall under the remit of Scottish Enterprise.

These agencies have also assumed control of the training functions previously run by the Manpower Services Commission and the Training Agency. Their appearance, after a short period of consultation at the end of the 1980s, represented a further restriction on the freedom of local authorities, eroding the traditional complementary role they enjoyed with the SDA and HIDB. There were thus early anxieties about the loss of consensus and partnership, as well as a lack of local accountability, as the local companies assumed the right to undertake economic development activity and organise training within their areas. These changes marked a departure from a market modified approach to one which was more centrally controlled in finance and planning, and reflected government frustration at the independence of the SDA as an economic operator and, it has been suggested, for claiming the credit for Scottish inward investment. It was also a response to pressure from business interests wishing to take control of the resources of the SDA and the Training Agency (Danson *et al.* 1989: 558). This approach has been compared to American initiatives on local development in the 1980s where the lack of private investment and public funding curtailment increased inequality. The assumption that employers will pay for training from augmented profit suggests a more optimistic scenario than any which has prevailed in the United Kingdom during the past century. Fragmentation will also disadvantage rural communities because of difficulties encountered in establishing local agencies, and the reduced funding levels will have a knock-on effect by reducing aid from the European Community where investment has to be matched with equal outlays from the recipient country. 'In effect, Scotland is being offered not devolution to locally-controlled consortia but rather a threat of direct rule by Sheffield (the Training Agency) and London (the DTI)' (Danson *et al.* 1989: 562).

The development of interventionist government generated an institutional network in Scotland through which that policy could be delivered. The emergence of the Scottish Office gave Scotland a separate and distinctive network which was different from the English regions. It provided a vehicle for lobbying in Westminster which areas like the west midlands and the north did not possess. The increased allocation of resources to the Scottish Office as the century progressed gave a measure of independence, and the delivery of policy through a network of agencies gave the Scottish Office substantial control. At first sight this structure appears to have given Scotland both some measure of policy independence as well as control over provision. But some observers have stressed the limitations of this structure, suggesting that the allocation of Scottish affairs to the Scottish Office encouraged other government departments to ignore Scotland, especially with regard to the distribution of government contracts. The recent preference of the Ministry of Defence for Devonport over Rosyth may reflect this as well as the anxieties of government backbenchers. It is also true, of course, that the final word on policy has been and remains determined by the party in government at Westminster.

Chapter 8

Government policy: implementation and effects

Economic intervention: regional policy

The impact of central government policy on Scotland has been most obviously manifest through regional policy which, initially, was concerned to modify imbalances in unemployment by facilitating the movement of labour away from the industrial blackspots. The Industrial Transference Board, set up in 1928, was intended to retrain labour and provide assistance to move workers to new employment. A more specifically regional policy emerged in the 1930s with the identification of four special areas with particularly high levels of unemployment together with an undertaking to effect their regeneration. One of these areas was in Scotland and comprised Clydeside and North Lanarkshire, although Glasgow was excluded. It received a very limited amount of financial assistance within a highly restricted remit such that the Scottish commissioner spent much of his budget on sewerage schemes. But the special areas development implicitly recognised a need to bring work to the workers as well as helping workers to move to find work. It is generally recognised that the impact of these initiatives was very limited, the number of new factories opened in all the special areas together being far outnumbered by the openings in prosperous Greater London which stood outside the assistance programme (McCrone 1969: 101). Only in 1937 were the commissioners for special areas allowed to offer subsidies to firms to provide work in their areas, as well as low interest loans.

After 1945 regional policy became primarily focussed on efforts to reduce unemployment in the areas where declining heavy industry was concentrated by relocating employment from other parts of the United Kingdom as well as by attracting jobs from abroad. This policy had its roots in wartime planning, and was based on the Distribution of Industry Act 1945 which set the framework for the following quarter of a century. The special areas were renamed development areas and expanded, so that Glasgow was now included in the Clydeside area. Dundee also became a development area as did, in 1948, the Inverness and Dingwall area as a focal centre for industrial development in the Highlands. The areas receiving assistance were rescheduled again in 1960, and the crucial requirement for inclusion became a high level of unemployment, which was defined as 4.5 per cent of the insured population. This change extended the Scottish development areas to include most of the Highlands and Islands. Perthshire was excluded, as well as a large area of the north east around Aberdeen. With a change of government in the middle of the decade came a further change. The new development areas defined in 1966 included all of Scotland, except Edinburgh, There were also special development areas, three in Scotland, which were primarily localities with a declining coalfield. These were able to provide additional incentives and rent free premises, building grants and subsidies.

The main thrust of postwar policy was to control the distribution of industry, using building licences to redirect new establishments towards development areas by refusing Industrial Development Certificates (IDC) in prosperous areas. The Board of Trade, which was given responsibility for the programme, was also able to build factories in development areas, to reclaim derelict land, provide some basic services and, with Treasury consent, make loans. General economic recovery in the 1950s, and a change of government, meant that regional policy was pursued with little vigour until the economic climate deteriorated towards the end of the decade. With the extension of development districts went a substantial increase in spending on factory buildings, loans and grants, from £5 million per year through the 1950s to £37 million by the early 1960s (Brown 1972: 288). This phase also witnessed the diversion of motor industry expansion away from its traditional locations in the west midlands and south east to Merseyside and central Scotland. Additional incentives in development areas included a scheme whereby profits could be written off against depreciation over time at any rate specified by the firm. Investments in plant and machinery were also eligible for a ten per cent grant, conditional on job creation, and the building grant scheme was simplified and increased in value. The 1966 legislation provided investment grants in development areas for business worth 40 per cent of the total outlay, twice the rate available elsewhere. Such firms also received advantageous terms for rentals, additional loans and grants, and help to train workers. Local authorities received aid for environmental improvement and the reclamation of derelict land. 'Taken together the provisions and their administration represented the most massive injection of resources in favour of the old "depressed areas" and a clear reinforcement of the dominance of the Board of Trade, and of the distribution of industry approach in Labour's regional policy' (Parsons 1988: 162).

In 1967 the regional employment premium was introduced, a cash subsidy of £1.50 per male worker employed in manufacturing in the development areas as well as a rebate on selective employment tax which had been imposed to 'shake' workers out of services into manufacturing. This reflected a change in strategy away from the redirection of industry towards the creation of an environment favourable for economic growth. But it also caused a concerted outcry against the advantages conferred by those who represented what were defined as intermediate areas. As their name suggests, these were locations which were largely excluded from aid although they suffered from substantial economic problems albeit less severely than the most seriously disadvantaged areas.

The main impact of regional policy in Britain was felt in the 1960s and 1970s In the 1950s it was essentially passive and from 1979 onwards it was systematically reduced in accord with the free market philosophy of the new administration. It has been estimated that in the period of active regional policy between 1960 and 1981 some 450,000 jobs were created in the development areas which survived at the end of that period. (Moore *et al.* 1986: 9). Assuming a regional multiplier of 1.4 a further 180,000 service sector jobs would be created making a total of 630,000 surviving jobs, many from the 1960s. Most of them were established in four main regional beneficiaries, Northern Ireland, Wales, Scotland and the North. Even so, this fell far short of providing a solution to the high levels of unemployment in these regions. In Scotland the combination of natural increase in the labour force, a rise in the participation ratio, and the decline of employment in traditional manufactures meant there was a substantial increase in demand for work even after the loss of some 350,000 migrants between 1950 and 1981. The inflow of new jobs was needed simply to prevent the unemployment rate actually rising.

During the period of passive regional policy in the 1950s the growth rate of Scottish manufacturing employment was close to its long-term expected trend given the structure of the economy, whereas in the active phase of policy during the following decade growth moved well above that rate. Much of the benefit to Scotland came from actual transfers not from the expansion of indigenous companies. In the 1950s the rate of new openings was very low, the benefits gained from the factory building programme of the late 1940s were no longer available, and the IDC controls on building in the prosperous regions were in abeyance. Revival in the 1960s returned with the reapplication of IDC controls and an active relocation programme, the number of moves increasing from 50 to 273 in the respective decades (Moore and Rhodes 1974: 218–23). Overall, it was estimated, Scotland gained a net addition of between 34,000 and 38,000 jobs in the 1960s with a further 12,000 to 15,000 created from indigenous firms. With indirect multiplier effects added a final gain of 70,000 to 78,000 jobs has been estimated. But this was only about one third of the jobs required to bring the unemployment rate and activity rate in Scotland to the same levels as those found in the south east and midlands. The effect of regional policy was to stabilise the rate of unemployment in the face of massive job losses in the heavy industries. It was also extremely expensive, as all estimates of job creation policies indicate.

There was little consistency between various phases of regional policy. In the early 1960s location controls were tight while expenditure was low, while in the latter half of the decade expenditure increased and controls were relaxed, a phase which continued on a larger scale through the 1970s. This explains, in part, why a larger proportion of the moves away from the South East actually went to the adjacent East Anglia and South West regions rather than to the assisted regions. Even so, recent estimates suggest that the majority of moves to the main development areas, including Scotland, were the result of regional policy, and that locational controls were more effective than investment incentives. For Scotland 81 per cent of the 264 manufacturing establishment gains between 1960–77 were the result of policy (Twomey and Taylor 1985: 261, 273–4).

The movement of factories into the major development areas between 1966 and 1978 indicated that Scotland and the North fared about the same, less successfully than Wales but better than Northern Ireland. In total Scotland secured 276 inward factory moves with an induced employment creation of 39,000 jobs (Moore *et al.* 1986: 56–8). The relative shortfall of jobs, defined as the sum of net outward migration plus the change in unemployment above the average for the United Kingdom, was lower in Scotland in the 1970s than it had been in the previous two decades. It was equivalent, on average, to 2.6 per cent of the labour force compared to 7.1 per cent in the 1960s, while net outward migration fell by half (Moore *et al.* 1986: 78). There were substantial gains from regional policy in these two decades, most of which came from regional invest-ment incentives (307,000 out of 450,000 jobs) and IDC controls (74,000 jobs). But the cost was considerable at £42,000 per job to the Exchequer and a total outlay between 1966–76 of £10,028 million (Moore *et al.* 1986: 10–11).

From the 1930s the crux of the economic problem in Scot-land was perceived as the combined effect of declining heavy industry and the failure of more modern forms of manufac-turing to flourish. Regional policy sought to tackle this prob-lem by attracting new industry to Scotland which, in turn, would bring about the revival of traditional activities. The boldest of these efforts was manifest in the attempt to create an indigenous motor car industry which, it was hoped, would revive demand for the Scottish steel industry and thence generate new industrial growth in central Scotland in the 1960s. The expansion of the previous decade in the motor industry meant that all the constitutent producers had made contingency plans for increased capacity by the late 1950s. The government was anxious to induce the motor companies to make this investment in the development areas to create employment in Wales, Scotland and Merseyside, while the trade unions were prepared to accept lower wage rates in these areas in exchange for such employment creation. The growth of a motor industry in Scotland was intended also to generate an increased demand for strip steel. The establishment of Ravenscraig in 1958, under strong government pressure, was intended to supply this demand from within Scotland. Board of Trade finance helped Pressed Steel to develop car body production capacity in an old steelworks at Linwood near Paisley in 1959. In the following year, the Rootes group was induced to set up a small but fully integrated motor plant at Linwood, thus completing the requisite economic linkages. Even so, Rootes was only induced to undertake this when refused IDCs to build the required plant on a 200 acre site owned by the company in Coventry (Wilks 1988: 78). The Scottish motor industry was, therefore, a creation of the government. But the Rootes plant was too small to exploit the economies of scale so vital for motor manufacture, and it was located at too great a distance from its principal component suppliers. As one critic of the policy observed, 'Clearly the government was prepared to trade off efficiency in the highly competitive international motor industry for lower regional employment rates'

(Dunnett 1980: 79). Dispersal of production without related rationalisation was bound to increase production costs and cut competitiveness.

All these strategies were pursued in the expectation of sustained industrial expansion. But Linwood was not successful. Industrial relations were very poor. Established forms of work in central Scotland and Merseyside had been hard but varied. Their replacement with easier but boring and repetitive work did not provide an easy or attractive exchange for the workers. The level of performance of the workforce turned out to be poorer than expected by the employers and led to redundancies and short-time working, which further eroded morale, within a decade. The Hillman Imp which was manufactured at Linwood was a poorly designed vehicle aimed at a market in which demand was changing in favour of larger cars, so that the expected growth in production and employment was not realised. The outcome was an appalling record for strikes and an almost unbelievably poor productivity rate.

By the mid 1970s Chrysler UK, which had acquired control of Rootes in the mid 1960s, was facing closure. The company was a massive exporter so that closure would have caused balance of payments problems, entailed considerable job losses, and threatened almost one fifth of British car output. The government thus instituted a rescue package which saved 5,500 of the 7,000 jobs at Linwood. The Scottish plant lost a lower share of its total employment than the two Coventry plants, even though the list of voluntary redundancies at Linwood was oversubscribed, and this caused much ill feeling in the midlands. Several explanations have been offered for this respite, most of which have been of a political nature, including fear of the SNP which had been highly successful in recent elections, the threat to the credibility of the recently established

Scottish Development Agency, and of the Secretary of State for Scotland who was closely associated with the policy. But reprieve for Linwood was only temporary. By the early 1980s Chrysler UK had been purchased by Peugeot whose expressions of goodwill regarding the maintenance of production turned out to be as empty as the controls imposed on the company by the government. The general belief in the industry that Peugeot was primarily interested in securing the dealerships appeared to be vindicated when Linwood finally closed in 1981. This, in turn, reduced the viability of Ravenscraig and only direct government intervention prevented its closure in 1982. Most observers have not been impressed by this particular example of state intervention, and it has been described as 'one of the most dismal failures of half-hearted interventionism' (Wilks 1988: 258). It also cost some ten million pounds to demonstrate that regional policy was 'more complicated than the setting up of new factories and the relocation of plants' (Dunnett 1980: 107).

By the 1970s the concern with unemployment which underlay regional policy was giving way in the perception of politicians and public to the new threat of inflation. This brought a major redirection in policy in which regional concerns were substantially downgraded. This policy was, however, also subject to the short-term constraints which have always preempted decisions in British government. The 1970 administration sought to make regional policy more selective, reducing IDC controls and phasing out the regional employment premium in favour of a growth point strategy. But rising unemployment in 1971 led to the establishment of special development areas, including Glasgow, which were favoured with public works projects. More grants and subsidies were made available in the following year, and the assistance to

Upper Clyde Shipbuilders ran counter to the avowed strategy of not helping 'lame ducks'. In 1972 location controls in the development areas were ended, and assistance was adjusted in favour of providing investment grants for plant, machinery and buildings. The old policy format lingered on under the subsequent Labour administration, and the regional employment premium was retained until its final demise in 1977, while new development agencies were set up in Scotland and Wales.

Besides the increase in inflation, traditional regional policy was undermined by the growing awareness of urban dereliction in regions outside those favoured for development, as manifest in the Notting Hill riots in 1976 which were a prelude to similar outbreaks in Toxteth, Brixton and St Pauls in the 1980s. It was also fundamentally at variance with the aims of the Conservative administration which came to power in 1979 pledged to free market solutions and the reduction of public spending. Between 1979 and the mid 1980s major reforms were introduced in regional policy. Development area boundaries were redrawn to reduce the proportion of the national labour force covered by them from 47 per cent to 15 per cent. Selective financial assistance remained only on a much diminished level, falling by half in the 1980s (Table 6). Restrictions on industrial building were eased outside assisted areas and abolished in intermediate areas. Industrial development certificates disappeared. A substantial cut in regional aid in 1984 was linked with a switch in emphasis in favour of concentrating on black spots by reducing the number of tiers of eligibility. Automatic grants were cut, and grants for plant and machinery disappeared. In 1988 the government abandoned automatic aid in favour of a case-by-case approach returning, it has been suggested, to the aims and approach of the 1930s

Table 6 Expenditure in Scotland on regional preferential assistance to industry

	1982/83	1983/84	1984/85	1985/86	1986/87	1987/88	1988/89	1989/90	1990/91	1991/92	1992/93
Scottish Development Agency/Scottish Enterprise	46.4	43.6	23.3	23.8	20.2	20.5	18.2	23.5	28.1	23.9	9.3
Regional selective assistance	20.1	24.7	31.7	48.1	35.4	38.3	38.0	40.7	68.2	63.7	59.2
Regional development grant	287.3	143.0	109.2	107.5	170.2	78.0	76.9	60.1	44.8	14.9	11.7
Highlands and Islands Development Board/ Highland Enterprise	15.6	17.3	22.9	17.6	16.6	16.4	18.1	18.3	18.1	20.3	20.5
Total gross expenditure £m	369.4	228.6	187.1	197.0	242.4	153.2	151.2	142.6	159.2	122.8	103.4

Sources: Scottish Office 1987. *Scottish Abstract of Statistics*, 16. p. 186.
Scottish Office. 1990. *Scottish Abstract of Statistics*, 19. p. 172.
Scottish Office. 1993–94. *Scottish Economic Bulletin*, 48. p. 84.

(Parsons 1988: 179). Selective financial assistance was to be provided only for those projects which otherwise would not be funded. But some of the new developments, such as LIS, were considerably successful: 'Even when the gross jobs planned by inward investment companies are discounted by one third as experience suggests they should, the inward investment efforts over the past decade have probably contributed to the attraction of some 50,000 jobs to Scotland' (Hood 1991: 13). Furthermore, by 1984, the efforts of the SDA had secured 3,200 jobs in the GEAR project, together with 800 houses built by the private sector and a further £50 million invested by business in plant, machinery and property.

In the 1980s the government sought a more selective and cost efficient regional policy. By the end of the decade half of all regional aid took the form of urban assistance as part of a general trend towards localism, including initiatives by local authorities. The new policy was characterised by the introduction of enterprise zones in 1980. Firms locating in such areas were exempt from local rates and development land tax. There were four such zones in Scotland: at Clydebank following the closure of the Singer plant and at Invergordon following the closure of the British Aluminium smelter, on Tayside and Inverclyde, both areas of high unemployment. The 1988 legislation introduced two new types of grant, one for small firms with up to 25 employees offering a 15 per cent investment grant to a maximum of £15,000 or a 50 per cent innovation grant to a maximum of £25,000, and consultancy grants for intermediate firms with less than 500 employees. Emphasis had clearly switched to helping inner city areas.

Membership of the European Community from 1973 onwards entitled the United Kingdom to receive aid from the European Community Regional Development Fund (ERDF) which was started in 1975 to help correct regional imbalances resulting from structural change and manifest in variations in unemployment. It offered grants for physical investment projects in special areas. Regional policy in the European Community moved in the same direction as that in the United Kingdom in the 1980s, offering more assistance to small firms and to depressed areas. By 1988 the fund was worth a little less than 10 per cent of the entire community budget and the bulk of funds expended in Britain and elsewhere were allocated to infrastructure developments. In 1988 it was determined that the ERDF would be doubled by 1992 in response to the creation of a single market. But funds for British regions were restricted by cuts in real spending by the United Kingdom government because assistance from ERDF required that much of its aid be matched by the host government.

Economic intervention: competition and industry

There has been a substantial and unavoidable overlap between regional policy and industrial policy in the postwar years, although the latter does have some distinctive and separate elements. One major theme running through industrial policy has been the desire to increase competitiveness by removing restrictive practices and controlling monopolies and mergers, although these aims were subject to modification on other grounds, and the final decision rests in the hands of the Secretary of State. In 1982, for example, the proposed take-over of Anderson Strathclyde of Motherwell, a mining engineering company and the third largest engineering company in Scotland at the time, by Chartered Consolidated was referred to the Monopolies and Mergers Commission. It advised against the merger on the grounds that it would have an adverse effect on employment. But the government overturned this decision and allowed the merger to proceed in 1983 (Swales 1983: 191).

Equally characteristic has been the pattern of erratic interventionism, as evidenced in the postwar history of shipbuilding. By the 1960s the industry was in a state of near collapse. The Geddes Report, commissioned by the Labour administration, recommended both mergers and reorganisation together with suggestions for improving the poor industrial relations. The government was keen to sustain employment, and stepped in to save the Fairfield yard on the Clyde when it collapsed in 1965, a move which was perceived by the new Department of Economic Affairs as 'a quite new partnership not only between Government and private enterprise but now between Government, private enterprise and the trade unions' (Strath 1987: 121). But while labour relations at Fairfield improved, the industry continued to be riven by industrial action as the many fragmented trade unions fought to protect their established positions as well as to increase pay. In 1971, under the Conservative administration, Upper Clyde Shipbuilders went into liquidation, and this stimulated a work-in by the labour force in the company's five yards to prevent closure and the resultant unemployment. Although the government had declared itself to be opposed to supporting lame ducks, it agreed to the restructuring of the company and provided the finance for the firm which emerged, Govan Shipbuilders. The power of the trade unions in this period, and the widespread priority given to curbing unemployment in political circles, is further reflected in the agreement made between union leaders and Marathon to enable the latter to take over the John Brown yard at Clydebank in 1972 for offshore fabrication work. The unions made an agreement that there would be no strikes provided jobs were safeguarded, and the government offered a

£12 million subsidy for the venture (Strath 1987: 127–8). But the basis for conflict remained. Trade unions expected government to provide subsidies to save jobs, company owners wished to retain their independence, conflict about wage rates and demarcation seemed endless, and the industry continued to be hopelessly uncompetitive in world markets. Nationalisation in 1977 did bring some improvement in labour relations with a single wage bargaining agreement, and demarcation disputes diminished in the 1980s when government support was reduced to expose the industry more overtly to market forces, resulting in an even more rapid contraction. The prevalence of political ideology, of all shades, together with historically bad labour relations, appears to have prevented any serious effort to address fundamental problems in the industry until it was far too late to arrest the process of decline.

The contraction in regional assistance towards the end of the 1970s, which has continued during the past fifteen years, was linked to the shift of government strategy for economic rejuvenation from intervention to strenuous support for competition, especially manifest in attempts to stimulate the latent energies of small businesses. It was further spurred by a shift in public and political perceptions by which inflation appeared more threatening than unemployment. In 1983 the Department of Industry issued a document outlining aims and policies for industry, which focused on profitability, competitiveness and the promotion of technological advance. One important new venture was the loan guarantee scheme introduced in 1981 which provided 80 per cent guarantees for loans, while the business start-up scheme gave relief on income tax up to £100,000 invested in a single year. Scotland has not been particularly successful in attracting funds from such schemes, securing only £7 million, equivalent to 4 per cent of United

Kingdom investment, between 1981–82 and 1986–87 (Bowen and Mayhew 1991: 91). At the same time planning constraints on small businesses were reduced as were the thresholds for IDCs.

During the 1980s the SDA became more commercially oriented and its financial obligations were revised. It was required to realise, over a five year period, a rate of return equivalent to the cost of its own borrowing from the government. It was also confined to making investments in circumstances in which private sector funding was unavailable, and needed the permission of the Secretary of State for investments over one million pounds. The lease of factories had to be at market valuations which, in derelict areas, were sometimes less than construction costs. In 1982 the agency was charged with an obligation to secure a rental income on premises over a three year period equal to a predetermined return on capital investment, set initially at 7.3 per cent (McCrone 1985: 240). It was also required to make a surplus from the entire industrial estate and factory provision programme equal to a target set by the Industry Department of Scotland. Eventually the SDA was obliged to sell off factory space in the industrial estates and dispose of the bulk of its property to the private sector at the end of the decade, thus terminating the provision of advance factories. But the agency became trapped between the fulfilment of aims which conflicted. 'Yet again there emerges the principle of the exposure of a public body to operating at the margin in the endeavour to take major initiatives, while at the same time managing risk in an acceptable manner' (Hood 1991: 16). It thus attracted adverse comment for involvement with risky projects like the Scottish Exhibition and Conference Centre and the Glasgow Garden Festival.

During the 1980s enterprise trusts played an important part

in providing local development services. The formation of Scottish Enterprise in 1991, bringing together the SDA and the Training Agency, the main agents delivering its services, and the local enterprise companies (LEC) threatens the future of the trusts. The resources made available to the LECs established them as the main agency for delivering economic policy. The development trusts brought together local authorities and the SDA under private sector leadership, so that by 1990–91 they received 19.5 per cent of their income from local authorities, 18.6 per cent from the SDA, 27.5 per cent from the private sector and the balance from earned income (Hayton 1992: 672). The funding power of the LECs has meant that the trusts have now become their operatives.

There have also been a number of local initiatives, such as Drumchapel Opportunities which was established in 1988 in one of the more disadvantaged of the peripheral housing estates in Glasgow. It emerged from a joint initiative from the local authorities in the area to secure jobs and revive the local economy. It obtained funding from the European Social Fund, Strathclyde Regional Council and the Scottish Office, with smaller contributions from Glasgow District Council, SDA, the Department of Employment and the private sector, making a budget of £1.6 million by 1990–91 (Turok 1992: 200). Most of the outlay was expended on training courses, although travel to interviews was subsidised as was, in the short term, travel to work. In sum the project succeeded in securing work for about 1,000 local residents in 1990.

Social intervention: housing

Just as government was drawn into economic management by a combination of specific problems and a change in public perceptions about the acceptability of reliance on market forces, so it was drawn into responding to a variety of social problems. One of these, and the problem which had a particularly great importance for Scotland, was housing provision. Prior to the First World War, government legislation had been mainly permissive. From 1866 onwards, for example, the City Improvement Trust in Glasgow had the power to purchase and destroy slum property, although it did little to replace the buildings which were demolished and by 1914 had contributed little more than 2,000 houses to a total stock of over 180,000 (Butt 1971: 63). Prior to the First World War the public sector as a whole made little contribution to Scottish housing, providing accommodation for only 1 per cent of families in 1913 (Rodger 1986: 183). The Royal Commission, which reported in 1917, described the appalling state of Scottish housing. But even more important than the catalogue of deprivation compiled was the view that any satisfactory solution could not be achieved through the operation of market forces.

> We are driven to the conclusion that the sources and forces that were available for the provision of working-class houses had ... failed to provide anything like a sufficiency of houses, and that in particular they had failed to provide houses of a reasonable standard of accommodation and habitability.
>
> ... Private enterprise was practically the only agency that undertook the building of houses, and most of the troubles we have been investigating are due to the failure of private enterprise to provide and maintain the necessary houses sufficient in quantity and quality (Royal Commission on Housing: 292).

Legislation passed in 1919 obliged local authorities to survey housing shortages and submit plans to Whitehall for their elimination, the costs to be shared between central and local government. The legislation imposed on local authorities an obligation to provide and manage housing, the financial burden being limited to the product of a nominal 0.8 pence levy on the rates. Central government undertook an open-ended commitment to pay the residual costs which clearly placed overall responsibility for improvement on the state. In fact, government involvement had already taken a major step forward in 1915 by freezing rents at the levels which were effective at the outbreak of war. Given wartime inflation this was not unreasonable, but it allowed rents to be set by political and social rather than economic considerations. Thus began, in earnest, the creation of the public housing sector.

Between 1920 and 1992 over 1.65 million houses were built in Scotland, almost a third of them by the private sector whose contribution was heavily concentrated in the most recent past (Figure 12). Between the wars, housebuilding in Scotland was dominated by the public sector which provided 67 per cent of new houses compared to 25 per cent in England and Wales, although the rate per head of population was little different (Baird 1954: 205). But over half the public sector housing in Scotland was built between 1945 and 1970, a total of over 650,000 houses. It is difficult to estimate precisely the contribution of central government, but it clearly was substantial. Between the wars the contribution of central government appears to have been about twice that of the local authorities, and after the war rather more than that. Estimates for the 1950s suggest a contribution to total costs made by central government in excess of 40 per cent. If this is assumed to be a long-run minimum, then the inference would be that central government funding paid for some 450,000 public sector houses in the twentieth century in Scotland, equivalent to more than 20 per cent of the current housing stock. This is certainly

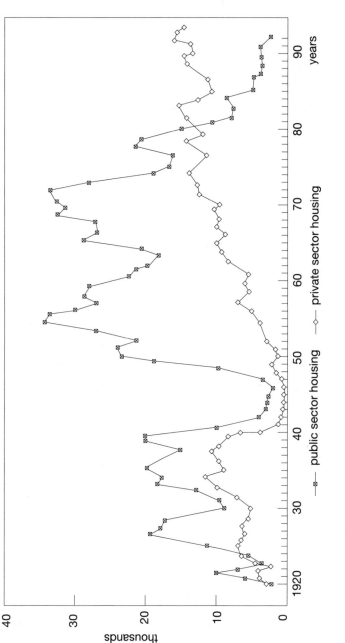
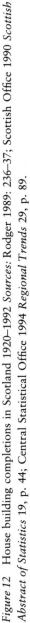

Figure 12 House building completions in Scotland 1920–1992 *Sources:* Rodger 1989: 236–37; Scottish Office 1990 *Scottish Abstract of Statistics* 19, p. 44; Central Statistical Office 1994 *Regional Trends* 29, p. 89.

a modest estimate, and excludes special subsidies and slum clearance transfer payments.

The massive demand for new housing in Scotland in the twentieth century reflected the peculiar neglect of the past both in the quality of housing provided and the extent of over-crowding. A survey taken in 1935 revealed that one house in four was overcrowded in Scotland compared to one in twenty-six in England and Wales according to the rather complex for-mula used. But, defining two persons per room as the maximum level acceptable, in 1931 some 35 per cent of Scots lived above this level compared to less than 7 per cent of people south of the border (Baird 1954: 197). While the dis-parity diminished in the first half of the century it still remained clearly marked. In 1951, the respective percentages were 15.5 and 2.2. In the 1930s the worst overcrowding was in the industrial towns in the west where Coatbridge, Port Glas-gow, Clydebank and Motherwell had overcrowding in over 40 per cent of their housing stock (Adams 1978: 176). Other mea-sures, such as persons per house or persons per room, indicate similar disparities. The absolute number of Scots living in one or two rooms was greater than in England and Wales in 1951, although access to facilities like piped water, fixed baths and water closets showed less variation.

At the end of the Second World War, Scotland still faced a massive deficit in housing provision as a result of continuing overcrowding, war damage, and newly-formed households, amounting to some half a million houses with almost as many again requiring sanitation and water supply improvements (Gibb 1989: 157). This was increased by the policy of popula-tion dispersal from the centres of major cities to peripheral estates, such as Castlemilk, Easterhouse, Drumchapel and Pollok in Glasgow, as well as further afield to Cumbernauld and Kilsyth, East Kilbride, and Irvine in the west, Glenrothes in the east, and Livingston in central Scotland. In the 1950s Glasgow embarked on a major building programme, and demolished 268,000 dwellings between 1955 and 1972 in the process. For a quarter of a century after 1945 there existed a political consensus in favour of massive public investment in housing, characterised by the construction of tenements in greenfield sites, of three and four apartments, and by a more centrally controlled provision of overspill housing and the demolition of inner city slums.

A larger share of Scottish housing dates from 1945 than is the case in England and Wales, compensating to some degree for the lower building rate between the wars. There has also been a belated transition towards owner-occupied housing; although the share of total housing which was owner-occupied in Scotland was only 55 per cent in 1993 compared to 67 per cent in England. This was a far lower proportion than could be found in any other part of the country, even though it had increased markedly in the 1980s from 36 per cent in 1981 (*Regional Trends* 29: 87). Private house building was sustained in Scotland through the 1980s with close to 20,000 units started each year. Public sector building, reversing a long expansive phase actually contracted whereas in earlier decades public sector housing had far outstripped private sector building. Part of the transformation of ownership was brought about by the sale of council houses usually to sitting tenants. While the stock of dwellings increased only slightly in the decade 1979–89 from 1.98 million to 2.10 million units, the owner occupied sector increased from 0.70 million to 1.03 million while the public rented sector, including SSHA, later Scottish Homes, and new town corporation housing as well as council housing, declined from 1.07 million dwellings to 0.88

million (*Scottish Abstract of Statistics* 19: 44). This radical change in housing provision was, of course, also a direct effect of government policy.

Central government contributed to housing construction through a system of subsidies, the rate and nature of which underwent numerous changes. The initial legislation of 1919 limited the financial contribution of the local authority while leaving the Exchequer with an open-ended commitment to make up the deficit. This was soon reversed, a change stimulated in part by the rapid escalation in building costs resulting from a postwar shortage of skilled men and materials. The legislation which came into force in 1923 allowed local authorities to undertake house building and to claim back from the Treasury a subsidy on each house built. This provided the basis for assistance until the late 1950s.

Changes were made periodically to the terms of these subsidies usually relating to the size of the payment or the period of time for which it could be obtained. The 1923 subsidy was worth £6 per house, and it subsequently ranged between £3 and £9 between the wars although it was worth £12.50 in rural areas. The period for which the subsidy would be paid was originally set at 20 years, but was later increased to 40 and then 60 year terms.

Additional subsidies were offered to deal with specific problems. The 1930 Act provided a subsidy of £2.50 for each person rehoused within a slum clearance programme, while the 1935 Act defined, for the first time, a minimum standard of overcrowding and offered a subsidy for efforts to tackle this problem. Each of these subsidies was to be accompanied by a smaller contribution made by the local authorities from the rates. In 1954 slum clearance legislation offered half the loan charge for purchase of the slum property plus a subsidy of

£7.25 per house for 15 years. In 1938 legislation provided subsidies related to the size of house, intended to encourage the construction of larger properties with the bulk of the cost being borne by central government, rising from £10.50 for a three-apartment house to £13 for one with five or more apartments (Cramond 1966: 15–23). After the Second World War additional subsidies were introduced for the inclusion of lifts (£7 per block of four storeys or more) and for overcoming the effects of subsidence in mining areas, and for houses built at additional expense. The programme was extended to stimulate improvements to existing properties in both public and private sectors. The 1949 legislation offered local authorities a refund of 75 per cent of the annual loss incurred on improvements they carried out themselves, payable for 20 years, and 75 per cent of the annual loan charge for the same period payable on grants made by local authorities to private owners for improvements (Cramond 1966: 31).

Concern about the increasing cost of subsidies and the fact that the programme was demand-led, being determined by the level of activity of local authorities in housing provision, caused central government to seek ways of limiting spending in the 1950s. In 1957, for the first time, the Exchequer subsidy was cut to a flat rate of £24, although there were still special subsidies of £42 for overspill housing and £30 for housing for incoming industrial workers. In 1962, further legislation enabled the government to cut the level of subsidy within the currently agreed 60 year period. The boom period of public sector housing reached its final peak in 1970, undermined by the combined effects of high interest rates and central government spending restraints.

The urgency of the first phase of postwar development deferred the provision of amenities for shopping and leisure.

But the quality of housing led to later problems. One critic commented that,

> Building designs totally unsuited to the Scottish climate and to the mass incarceration of humanity were symptomatic of the lack of architectural conception and commitment, producing built environments of stultifying insensitivity and monotony. Flat roofs failed to shed heavy rainfall and acted as reservoirs for rainwater which percolated through inadequately sealed joints to the dwellings below. Cladding slabs were secured by ferrous pins which rusted rapidly in the climate and in the worst cases gave way entirely, hurling their half-ton burdens hundreds of feet to shatter on the paving slabs below (Gibb 1989: 168).

These faults were compounded by a lack of quality control both in the fabrication of components and in assembly which meant that many buildings were scheduled for demolition before the interest on the loans made for their construction was paid. Others are more inclined to blame the arrogance of planners and local authorities in formulating grandiose but inadequate plans.

As a result the 1970s witnessed a sharp shift in policy from construction to renovation. Legislation passed in 1969 widened the range of improvement grants and increased their value. By the 1972 legislation, Treasury grants covered 90 per cent of rent rebate and allowances. Subsequent legislation in that decade increased improvement grants, imposed minimum standards on local authorities, and gave support to housing associations. Under the new Conservative administration, in 1980 valuation procedures were set up by which council properties could be purchased, discounts of up to 60 per cent being available according to the length of tenancy, and these rights were further increased in 1986. The Housing Act of 1988 gave public sector tenants the right to have their tenancies transferred to new landlords, including private companies, housing associations and co-operatives. Under these programmes the housing situation changed drastically as 18.6 per cent of the public sector stock was sold in the 1980s.

The change in policy during the 1970s curtailed the new town programme. By 1976 Stonehouse had been demoted from new town status and plans were devised for redeveloping housing within Glasgow as an alternative strategy. This marked a secular decline in housing completions in the public sector which was reversed only briefly in the middle of the decade by a surge related to the growth of the oil industry. The housing support grant system started in 1978 gave firm central government direction to housing spending. By 1980 some 20,000 dwellings had been rehabilitated by the local authorities, the SSHA, and local housing associations. The desire to restrict public spending in the 1980s brought a sustained reduction in public sector housing expenditure. There was an overall loss of 30 per cent in Scotland between 1980 and 1984, less than in England and Wales, but more devastating in effect. While subsidies to the private sector increased, housing support grant fell sharply. This forced councils to increase rents, and shifted the liability on the public purse to housing benefit for which increasing numbers of people qualified. The continued deterioration in the quality of the housing stock (half a million houses were estimated to need treatment for damp in 1986), and the accelerated rate of household formation in the 1980s increased homelessness which was estimated to affect 1 per cent of families in 1986. From a radical perspective, it seemed that in the 1980s 'purposive, planned housing policy has been sacrificed to the primal urge of public spending reduction' (Gibb 1989: 181). This further increased the costs which would be incurred when renovation, rebuilding and new construction eventually resumed.

Government involvement in the housing market in pursuit of policies needed to ameliorate living conditions extended beyond the provision of subsidies for construction and renovation to the control of rents. The precedent was set during the First World War, and continued in the Rent Restriction Act of 1920 which pegged the contractual rent of controlled housing. This meant that any increase in the rates fell on the owner and reduced his return from renting the property. This consequently diminished any incentive to improve or even maintain the property, a constraint which did not apply in England and Wales. Under the 1919 legislation, the subsidy commitment of central government was open-ended and thus inversely related to rents. Subsequent legislation in 1923 and 1924 switched to fixed subsidies which put the onus for rent control onto the local authorities. The 1935 Act was based on the assumption that rents should be fixed at market values, and embodied the idea that only the disadvantaged should occupy public sector housing, but that rent rebates should be allowed to the poorest in society. After 1945 central government abandoned the control of rents which were left to the discretion of local authorities. It was in this postwar period that the real value of rents in Scotland fell well below the market value of many properties, and by the mid 1950s were half the rents of comparable properties in England and Wales. This led to increasing conflict between central and local government.

Local authorities, especially those which were controlled by a Labour administration, as many were in central Scotland, preferred to keep rents to a minimum. Indeed the provision of cheap housing had become a major part of the policy of the

Labour Party and underpinned its support in Scotland. Baird estimated on the basis of 1952 data that the local authority rents required to cover costs without any subsidy would be 4.5 times the actual rent charged (Baird 1954: 207–8). In fact average rents fell far short of the sum required to cover costs even when the subsidy was included. Another estimate, made in 1956 found that the annual loan and maintenance charges on a four-apartment house would be about £100 per annum. This was defrayed, in part, by an Exchequer subsidy of £42.25 and a rate contribution of £14.25 leaving a balance of £43.50 which should have been met by rental payments, although the average rent at the time was £18 (Cramond 1966: 39). Faced with such deficits, local authorities often chose to increase rates, seldom to increase rents. Another option was to run into debt. Glasgow had a net deficit of £1.1 million on its housing account by 1952–53.

In an attempt to force local authorities to stop subsidising their tenants by transfers from both ratepayers and central government, subsidies were reduced from the late 1950s. But the most drastic reductions were introduced by the Thatcher administration. The capital allocation grant fell by 25 per cent between 1979–80 and 1981–82, while the housing support grant, the fund through which central government supported council house rents, was cut to compel local authorities to increase rents. Total expenditure at constant prices fell from £14.8 million in 1976–77 to £7.5 million in 1989–90 for the United Kingdom as a whole. By the latter date, mortgage tax relief, which increased steadily, had reached £6.5 million. The growing reliance on capital receipts to fund housing programmes suggests they will continue to decline in real terms. Within public expenditure programmes, funding has switched almost completely from house building to renovation while expenditure has been linked to specific items. In real terms the housing subsidy fell in Scotland by 1989–90 to 15 per cent of its 1979–80 level, much of that drop coming in the first three years of the period. Even so, substantial subsidies remain in some public sector housing systems. In Glasgow at the beginning of the 1990s, subsidies meant that rents were only half the required market rents, with a subsidy per tenant of £1,174 which was far higher than in any of five English cities surveyed (Maclennan *et al.* 1991: 24–9, 44). But applications for housing from the homeless rose steadily and exceeded 27,000 households in 1989–90.

Policy and the Union

The effect of economic and social policy on Scotland can be clearly delineated. In addition to the benefits from transfer payments, positive over most of the century because of the excess of expenditure over taxation, Scotland gained from regional policy which redirected employment on a substantial scale in the 1960s and 1970s. There was also a net gain in employment from state support to nationalised industry and a large and clear social gain from housing policy. These benefits were modest between the wars when public expenditure was still limited, but became very substantial in the three decades following the Second World War. There followed a period of relative decline in the 1980s as government policy changed in favour of encouraging competitiveness and new firm formation. Ironically, it was in the early 1980s that Scotland suffered, almost certainly for the first time, a substantial net loss from redistribution policies within the Union in that expenditure from central government did not cover tax revenue paid, providing it is assumed that oil taxation should be credited to

Scotland's account.

Government policy has been important and influential throughout the century, and taxation and public expenditure have both risen to comprise almost half the national income. These changes alone indicate the far greater importance of the Union in Scottish affairs in the present century, and particularly since 1945, than was the case in the eighteenth or nineteenth centuries. While, on balance, the benefits appear to have outweighed the costs, certainly in regard to tax and expenditure, the importance of policy raises the question of whether an alternative strategy might have been better. Throughout the century, at least until the 1980s, independence would certainly have been more expensive than membership of the Union. The lower taxable capacity from lower wages and higher unemployment would have imposed a restraint either in the form of less public expenditure or in a higher tax rate than was actually experienced. This would have been needed in order to balance government accounts in the absence of transfer payments from the rest of the United Kingdom. In the 1970s the deficit by which identified public expenditure fell below taxation raised in Scotland ranged annually between 7 and 9 per cent of Scottish GDP. In general terms that scale of increase would have been required in revenue from taxation to achieve a balance. Furthermore the estimates for public expenditure include only the identifiable component, which is about 80 per cent of the total, and excludes any expenditure an independent government might make on defence or diplomatic services. An independent state would certainly have chosen to make some outlays of this type so that the tax increase to balance the government account would have been even greater than the 7–9 per cent indicated above. It seems improbable that independence would have allowed a greater level of public spending, either to assist industry or to increase welfare. The costs of the public sector housing subsidy alone would have imposed a crippling burden on an independent Scottish state.

If the balance of public finance firmly supported union until the very recent past, the 1980s brought a situation in which Scotland contributed more to the Westminster government than it received in return. This change was wrought entirely by the oil boom and the massive revenues which accrued to the Treasury in the first half of that decade. In that period, an independent Scotland would have been able to afford a substantial increase in public spending or enjoyed tax reductions on the basis of an average surplus on government account over five years which was equivalent to almost 30 per cent of national income. But by the end of the decade that windfall had ended with the decline in oil revenues, and the net deficit had been restored.

With the exception of the 1980s, therefore, it seems likely that the economic policy of an independent Scotland would have been severely constrained by fiscal limitations unless it could have achieved an extremely high, and historically unprecedented, rate of economic growth or supported a substantial deficit. The need to attract employment from overseas, including England, would have remained but would not have enjoyed the benefit of United Kingdom regional policy incentives. Such costs would also have fallen on the state. On the other hand there may have been some advantage to be gained by being freed from the heavy hand of the British Treasury, and the long-established primacy of deflationary policies to curb inflation, real or threatened, and to support the exchange rate. Such policies reflected the preference of financial interests which doubtless found an echo in Edinburgh as well as the City of London. But they were never sympathetic to the need for economic restructuring or industrial regeneration with ameliorating influences on unemployment. They have also entailed periodic waste of funds in the defence of untenable exchange rate parities long after they could be sustained, such as the massive losses incurred on Black Wednesday in September 1992 under the stewardship of a reluctant, and Scottish, Chancellor of the Exchequer.

The claim that the economic policy of an independent Scottish administration would have been at least as effective as that which was received from Westminster is an extremely modest one. It is, of course, possible that a Scottish government would become wedded to extensive military commitments or the attractions of tough exchange rate policies. But the claim that the policies of an independent regime would have been able to achieve a level of economic regeneration sufficient to overcome the deep structural weaknesses in the Scottish economy, or the widespread poverty, or the fiscal deficit, must be rated extremely doubtful. But the balance of benefit and loss is never stable nor constant. It is rather ironic that Scotland should have been able to generate such a large surplus on an independent public sector account in a decade when the transfer benefits for regional assistance were falling (Table 6). For the first time, in that decade it can be plausibly argued that an independent policy regime could have served Scotland better than that currently offered within the Union, although the financial basis on which it was founded was short-lived.

There exist other restraints on policy. There is at present no strand of opinion which perceives the future of Scotland other than as a member of the European Union. For the past twenty years United Kingdom membership has meant that government policy has been constrained by decisions made in Brussels either reluctantly, as in the case of the common agricultural policy, or enthusiastically, as in the firm and unyielding commitment to the fixed parities established under the exchange rate mechanism. Like the rest of the United Kingdom, Scotland has both gained and been restricted by such policies. Continued membership, universally accepted at present by all shades of political opinion, undoubtedly means that increasingly economic policy will be constrained by the aims and policies of this larger union. The scope for economic management outside the old Union might in future decades be no greater than that allowed by the new union. In that event, from an economic perspective, the question of whether Scotland should remain within the Union or withdraw from it may have little importance.

Part IV

Conclusion

Chapter 9

The balance sheet of the Union

The legacy of the past

Throughout the twentieth century, Scotland has undergone a difficult economic transition as the structures which constituted the basis of Victorian industrialisation were initially eroded and subsequently collapsed. Since that economy had been based on labour intensive production in heavy industries and located in central Scotland, the most painful experience of twentieth-century transition was manifest in unemployment in those industries and localities. Even lower population growth, outward migration and a stable workforce were not able to bring the unemployment down to acceptable levels. In part, this was due to the fact that the new jobs which were created were often in services rather than in manufacturing, for women rather than for men, for professional or semi-skilled workers rather than for skilled manual workers as in the Victorian era, and were often outside the areas of greatest unemployment. By 1991 unemployment stood at 220,000 people, an overall rate of 8.7 per cent in official statistics. This covered marked sex and regional variations, male unemployment standing at 11.5 per cent compared to 5.1 per cent for females. While male unemployment stood at 14.3 per cent in Strathclyde, and over ten per cent in Central, Fife and Tayside, in Grampian it was only 4.3 per cent (*Scottish Economic Bulletin* 45: 75). Overall regional unemployment rates ranged from 3.7 per cent in Grampian to 10.9 per cent in Strathclyde.

In fact regional variations in economic prosperity are now both greater and potentially more divisive than those between Scotland and the rest of the United Kingdom. In 1991 Scotland's GDP per head stood at 95.8 per cent of the national average. But this rate, which marked a sustained improvement over several years as Scotland missed the worst of the depression of the late 1980s, as it had missed the preceeding boom, concealed very substantial internal differences. While most Scottish regions fell well below the United Kingdom average, Grampian and Lothian came well above it. Grampian came second only to Central London while Lothian was placed seventh in the national hierarchy. The extent of disparity within Scotland is shown by expressing the same data against a benchmark of Strathclyde region (equal to 100) which houses almost half the Scottish population. Most Scottish regions fell within 2 per cent of the Strathclyde base, and only Fife 95.9 per cent and Borders 92.3 per cent were clearly below. But Lothian came 19.9 per cent above this baseline and Grampian 52.6 per cent above it. Scotland thus contains two of the most prosperous regions in the United Kingdom, which account for about 25 per cent of the Scottish population, while the rest of the country falls well below the national average by a margin of 10–20 per cent (*Regional Trends* 29: 177).

The variation in incomes between regions was mirrored by substantial variations between social groups. Even the benefits of the oil industry, great as they have been in generating some 50,000 new jobs mainly in the north east, have increased such disparities. In Aberdeen there have been significant redistributive effects which have brought loss as well as gain. The employment created favoured men rather than women and skilled middle class workers rather than others. While money wages rose substantially from well below to well above the United Kingdom average, there was also a sharp increase in the cost of living (Harris *et al.* 1986: 275). Rising house prices provided capital gains for those already in the market but made it increasingly difficult for first time buyers to enter. Council house occupiers were protected by the low rent policy of the District Council, but the power to limit the subsidy from the rates, acquired by the Scottish Office, eroded that protection from the mid 1980s onward. The subsidy paid to council house tenants was substantially less than that paid to the private sector in mortgage relief. The prosperity brought by the oil benefited the better off and those directly influenced by employment in the industry, but entailed redistributive losses for the weaker sections of the community not touched directly by the industry.

A more familiar and obvious picture of the enduring deprivation of parts of Scotland is shown by the fact that while Strathclyde region contained 44 per cent of all the census enumeration districts in Scotland in 1981, it also had 88 per cent of the most deprived and, within the region, much of the deprivation was concentrated in Glasgow. Measured against the poorest English cities Glasgow fared particularly badly in terms of overcrowding and large households (Pacione 1986: 1504). High levels of male unemployment were found in the major housing estates on the periphery of the city at Easterhouse, Drumchapel, Castlemilk and Pollok which were built in the two decades after 1945. An analysis of Easterhouse showed that the principal ingredients of multiple deprivation were large households, several children, male unemployment and single parent families. Many pensioners lived in poor circumstances. In fact almost one third of households with multiple deprivation in Scotland consisted of pensioners living alone.

> Although these dwellings are equipped with the basic amenities, other physical problems are evident, as in the mismatch between household size and house type leading to a high level of overcrowding ... Socially based problems, such as those related to unemployment, high proportions of permanently sick or disabled persons, and single-parent families are also over represented in areas of local authority housing (Pacione 1986: 1516).

As many academic studies have found, the poverty of Scotland has its origins in the workplace. Inadequate wages mean it is impossible to provide for sickness or retirement or ride out periods of unemployment.

While the Scottish economy has made considerable progress in restructuring and creating new prosperity since the Second World War, the size of that task was such that much remains to be achieved. By most economic and social indicators, as evidenced above, Scotland remains, with the exception of a few favoured locations, troubled by unemployment, poor housing and most other characteristic features of relative deprivation. The root causes of these problems lie in Victorian industrialisation and the twentieth-century readjustment necessitated by changed circumstances. The Union cannot legitimately be blamed for this. The structure of the Victorian economy in Scotland was very largely fashioned by the Scots themselves. The scale of the transition problem was such that it is highly unlikely that an independent Scottish government would have had the resources to manage that change any better than it actually was managed within the framework of the United Kingdom. Indeed the substantial transfer of resources to Scotland throughout almost the entire twentieth century considerably assisted that process of readjustment. It is, of course, possible to argue that the United Kingdom government itself could have managed change better. The policy preference for price stabilisation and protection of the exchange rate meant that industrial restructuring always enjoyed a low priority, and stands as an enduring weakness in policy (Tomlinson 1994). Many studies of British economic policy in the twentieth century have depicted it as characterised by a mixture of folly and incompetence (Pollard 1982). Together with other regions of the United Kingdom, Scotland has suffered the effects of that malaise.

The advantages of independence

While the benefits of the Union suggest that membership constituted the best economic option for Scotland almost continuously from 1707 until the very recent past, the changes in policy and the balance of tax and expenditure in the 1980s warrant reconsideration. There can be little doubt that Scotland is an economy both large enough and prosperous enough to sustain an independent existence within the framework of the European Union. Nor is there any obvious reason why an independent Scotland should not be allowed immediately to assume membership of that organisation. Independence should, therefore, be regarded as an entirely feasible option, both economically and politically. The strongest part of the case for independence, on economic grounds, must lie in the policy-making powers which would then be fully determined within Scotland. Even with a substantial measure of devolved decision-making and control over expenditure, as has developed over the past twenty years, central government policy is currently and properly determined at Westminster for the United Kingdom as a whole. While it is clear that Scotland gained substantially from regional policy in its most active phase in the 1960s and 1970s through the inward transfer of employment, it is equally true that the change in policy emphasis in the 1980s, favouring the competitively strong, was to the advantage of regions like the South East rather than to weaker regions like Scotland. Furthermore, as the SNP has argued, policies determined on the basis of the needs of the entire United Kingdom or of South East England are seldom equally suitable for Scotland. The deflationary policy package introduced in the late 1980s, which triggered the most recent recession, was a direct response to overheating in the South East which was itself a product of budgetary changes in mortgage tax allowances. It might also be added that the effectiveness of United Kingdom economic management has not been so impressive as to persuade pretenders that they would have great difficulty in performing as well or even better than Whitehall.

Apart from the determination of policy within Scotland, the same argument extends to embrace the notion that an independent country would secure better representation within the European Union, with a clearer strategy and more distinctive identity. In support of this contention, attention is often drawn to the success of the Republic of Ireland. Even the benefits which are gained, some have claimed, would have been achieved earlier under an independent administration.

The SNP is delighted that the whole of the Highlands and Islands is to qualify for European Community Objective 1 funding status, thanks largely to the efforts of the local Euro-MP and the regional council. However, the only reason why the Highlands and Islands did not qualify in the late 1980s was the absurd figures prepared by the UK Government, which suggested that the area was better off than Kent and East Anglia. Had Scotland been an Independent Member State of the EC, the Highlands and Islands would have long been enjoying the benefits of Objective 1 status (SNP, *Scottish Budget*: 11).

In the 1970s the economic case for independence relied heavily on the windfall revenues from oil. These were certainly substantial in the 1980s, greatly so for a few years in the middle of the decade, but while only about one fifth of the total reserves have been extracted the projected revenue returns are rather more modest than those realised in the early 1980s, tax revenues being estimated in the range £2–4 billion per annum through the present decade. The SNP budget estimates for independence still place considerable reliance on the revenues from oil which, it is assumed, would be divided according to the equidistance principle which 'involves charting a line which corresponds to equal distances from the landfall sites of each country involved. This demarcation would give Scotland some 90 per cent of the revenues from the Northern and Central Basins of the North Sea, and this is the assumption upon which our revenue projections are based' (SNP, *Scottish Budget*: 22). Thus the most recent projection, published in November 1993, relating to the tax year 1994–95 envisages an increase in expenditure of £1,688 million of which £1,200 million would be covered by additional oil revenues, the balance being made up from lower unemployment benefit payments as people are drawn back into employment, (an expectation which forms part of the argument and strategy of all political parties), and cancellation of Scotland's contribution to the Trident defence programme (SNP, *Scottish Budget*: 24–6). Revenue from oil would also provide Scotland with a higher rate of growth of GNP, it is claimed, making a difference of some £18 billion in national income by 1997, a sum equal to 1.5 times the annual budget of the Scottish Office (Salmond 1993: 20).

One clear benefit of securing the oil revenues, which are currently attributed to Scotland's trade figures, lies in the fact that there would be a surplus in the balance of trade and payments account. The problems of deriving a balance of payments for Scotland are well known. Much of Scottish trade has always passed across the border to England, but the absence of customs barriers means that it has passed unrecorded. Nor is there a separate currency whose fluctuations might presage weakness or strength as reflected in official reserves or the exchange rate. Using the Scottish Office input–output data, Dow constructed a balance of payments estimate for Scotland for 1979. This suggested a trade deficit worth £1,050 million (or £520 million if the Continental Shelf is included as part of Scotland). Scotland's share of the public sector deficit, assumed to be directly proportional to population, would be a £610 million net inflow although this is probably an underestimate given the weakness of the Scottish economy *vis-à-vis* the southern regions. But if the latter scenario is adopted, with the Continental Shelf included in Scotland, this item would be a net outflow of £1,703 million (Dow 1988: 20). There are no directly observable data for the other components of the current account, property income from abroad and private sector transfers. Oil revenues were, of course, modest in 1979, although earlier estimates of Scotland's trade balance show a persistent deficit. Recent and future projected balance of payments estimates, given oil, show Scotland clearly in surplus and thus delaying the balance of payments constraint on growth which has characterised the United Kingdom's experience in recent decades. The familiar stop–go pattern has been that growth stimulated consumer spending which then sucked in more imports, thence weakening the balance of payments. The corrective deflationary action instigated by the government to reduce the balance of payments deficit then snuffed out the growth, completing the cycle.

The economic case for independence thus depends on three central arguments: firstly that independent economic management could produce policies more suited to the Scottish economy and represent Scotland abroad more forcefully than Westminster and Whitehall; secondly that the revenues from oil and other forms of energy like hydroelectric power which make Scotland energy-rich can generate and sustain growth; and thirdly that 'Scotland is not and never has been a recipient of substantial Treasury largesse. Instead we have suffered a heavy penalty in lost growth and lost economic opportunity from the London connection' (Salmond 1993: 11).

The benefits of the Union

The case for the status quo is, to some degree, the converse of that for independence. Its strongest element lies in the fact that Scotland still enjoys in most years, even with the oil revenues, a net gain in public sector transfer payments. In view of the continued loss of active population by migration, the ageing population and poor housing provision which ensure the continued need for both social security help and economic regeneration for some decades to come, such support seems essential. Given the level of financial transfers which Scotland has enjoyed from the United Kingdom government, there is little doubt that independence would entail some considerable cost. In 1989–90 on the assumption of a long-run excess of 25 per cent in expenditure over revenues, the deficit was equal to

8.4 per cent of Scottish GDP. To maintain the same public expenditure an independent Scotland would have to increase the tax returns by 25 per cent or borrow a sum comparable to a large share of national income. If we modify these assumptions to the effect that Scotland received all the oil revenues paid in that year, there would still be an overall deficit on public spending equivalent to 1.8 per cent of GDP. This deficit could be eliminated by raising total tax revenue by about 5 per cent. The Scottish Budget estimated for 1991–92 for the SNP found that general government receipts, including oil revenues, fell 5 per cent short of general government expenditure commitments, leaving a notional Scottish public sector borrowing requirement of £1.1 billion (SCESR Budget: 1). An independent Scotland would have to cover that deficit, and would face extremely unpleasant policy choices in seeking to do so. A reduction in spending would be difficult, and highly unpopular, in view of rising and demand-led social security obligations, as indeed would the alternatives of increased taxation or public sector deficit. The scope to adopt the latter strategy would be further circumscribed if the price of a settlement of independence was that Scotland was burdened with a 'fair share' of the current United Kingdom public sector borrowing requirement deficit. It seems probable, therefore, that an independent Scotland would have some difficulty in maintaining and financing public expenditure at present levels, a necessity given the problems both of social deprivation and economic decline which still affect much of the country. This viewpoint would reject the third of the nationlist claims, that Scotland has not fared well in obtaining resources from Whitehall, and the evidence of twentieth-century history would certainly support that rejection. Outside the Union, twentieth-century Scottish structural readjustment would almost certainly have been weaker and slower. The unionist case would further suggest that devolution of control to the Scottish Office in recent decades has satisfactorily answered the demands for decentralised economic management, and add that oil revenues are unlikely to be sufficient to sustain or warrant independence.

Devolution?

The theoretical case for utilising local as opposed to central government is articulated in decentralisation theory which proposes that localities can best identify and supply the quantity of public services required, avoiding or reducing the deadweight loss incurred by provision determined by central government which will probably be too much for some and too little for others (Oates 1972: 35). Local government is better informed about the requirements of its citizens, finds it easier to monitor the activities of bureaucrats than national government and is better able to correct decisions made by imperfectly informed central administrations.

There are thus serious theoretical grounds for favouring devolution as well as the possibility that it might offer the best of both worlds, independence of choice and the benefits of transfers from central government. In any system of devolved government, including local authority administration, there must be fiscal autonomy. Any system which relies on central government to collect revenue and disburse it to local or regional governments in the form of grant allocations does not ensure that the transfers will be adequate or even as promised. The centralisation of British government in the 1980s and emasculation of local government by financial control is clear evidence of this. Devolution thus implies the abandonment of the unitary state (Hughes 1987: 21–2).

The critical problem involved in devolution lies in the detail of which taxes and powers should be devolved. Some taxes are unsuitable for regional devolution, like corporation tax which is best collected from large units, and which would be highly inconvenient for companies with operations in several regions if they were obliged to determine precisely where certain earnings were accrued. Vehicle excise duty could be devolved, but this would be disadvantageous to Scotland which has a relatively low vehicle ownership but a high level of road miles per head of population.

It is generally agreed that the most suitable taxes for devolved government are income tax, VAT and existing local authority taxation. Local or regional government, to have a sufficiently large and independent source of income, must have a wide tax base such as could only be provided by a local income tax. This might be achieved simply by splitting the existing income tax, at the basic rate of 25 per cent, into two components, with 15 per cent payable to central government and 10 per cent to a devolved assembly. The regional executive might be allowed to increase or reduce the devolved tax rate within say a limit of 3 per cent, so that the effective overall rate would fall in the range 22 to 28 per cent. In sum the budget of an assembly could comprise four elements, a block grant from central government as at present, a share of the local rates income, an assigned share of income tax and a share of VAT receipts relative to Scotland's share of the United Kingdom population (Heald 1990: 23, 48–9).

Three taxation models were identified in the 1989 consultative documents prepared by the Scottish Constitutional Convention. The first was a block grant payment similar to that currently paid to the Scottish Office, the second adopted the type of strategy favoured by Heald, while the third would give control over all taxation to an assembly which would pay national government for services such as defence. Heald is unenthusiastic about this latter possibility, noting the costs of administrative restructuring but mainly fearful of the threat to United Kingdom wide equalisation policies which have been so beneficial to Scotland (Heald 1990: 56). Scotland would be particularly at risk if there were any shift from taxes which are spent generally according to need to designated taxes which have to be spent in the region in which they are raised. Furthermore, it is usually argued that the redistributive function of taxation, for some its main purpose, is best fulfilled at national level. The imperfections of the central grant allocation system mean that, under devolution, it is almost certain that part of that redistribution function would have to be contained within the devolved component (Helm and Smith 1987: xix). Given Scotland's income and wealth inequalities, this could provoke political conflict. It is possible that devolution could actually produce a net loss, if independently raised and dedicated revenues failed to make up for 'lost' transfer payments. The final outcome would depend heavily on the terms under which devolution, especially of tax obligations and expenditure rights, were established.

The English perspective

The discussion has to this point considered the Union from an exclusively Scottish point of view. It is certainly true that most of the discussion on the subject since 1707 has been generated north of the border. The political success of the nationalists in recent decades, and the publicity they have attracted in Scotland, does not appear to have found any response, hostile or otherwise, in England. This is, perhaps, not surprising. As much the larger partner, the Union is perhaps of less concern than in Scotland and the desire for Scotland's oil, so ferociously trumpeted by the SNP in the 1970s, is probably less obvious a goal to the citizens of England than to their elected representatives. But as the problems of the United Kingdom economy remain unresolved, and the public finances remain at the centre of debate, this may change.

One obvious source of potential English disenchantment lies in the imbalance between public expenditure and taxation. The southern regions of England have paid for the economic and social subsidies paid to the weaker economic regions of the United Kingdom for at least the past thirty years. In the case of the large and highly prosperous South East this has been very expensive. A recent study has estimated the cost of such regional subsidies to London alone, suggesting that each household in the capital pays £1,790 per year more than it receives in benefits, an annual deficit of £8.2 billion. In the endless debate about who subsidises who and to what extent, this may be compared to the SNP claim that Ministry of Defence spending constitutes a subsidy of £7.85 billion to the South East (Rosie 1992: 16). Spokesmen for the metropolis are now asserting that too much public spending is devoted towards social welfare programmes and too little spent on crucial infrastructure and transport systems which are vital to London and which are in a state of rapid deterioration. Accordingly, they argue, the Government should take action to rebalance the tax and subsidy position by switching resources to infrastructure spending in the capital (Hutton 1993).

Historians have generally agreed that economic concerns were unimportant for the English in joining the Union in 1707, and that they were concerned primarily with potential military action against the French. This may now be a less pressing anxiety, even after the opening of the channel tunnel, so there does not seem any overwhelming need, other than sentiment, for the English to retain the Union. Even the loss of the oil revenues would have a relatively marginal effect on the residual United Kingdom economy given that this would be partly offset by reduced public expenditure commitments. Indeed the 1989–90 estimates which suggest that Scotland would have had a deficit of 1.8 per cent of GDP on public account even with oil revenues accredited indicate that Scottish independence would give the residual United Kingdom a small fiscal benefit. It may well be that the price of continued Union might entail some further curtailment of regional subsidies or a change in their composition. Early indications of this can be seen in pressure from southern MPs to have their constituencies assigned assisted area status in response to the recent recession which was felt most heavily in the southern regions. The decision to favour Devonport rather than Rosyth with defence contracts is a further indication of the increased pressure on government for economic assistance from its natural constituency.

It may be that opposition to the Union, or at least its regional redistributive effects will come from other quarters. While the southern regions may wish to reduce the scale of transfer payments, poorer regions like Wales and the North may wish to increase their share. There is little doubt that Scotland has fared better than either of these regions in recent decades but that they remain clearly poorer. Short's estimates for the 1970s show a clear disparity in favour of Scotland over these two lagging regions (Table 5). Furthermore there are today more localised areas of the United Kingdom which fall much further below the national GDP per head average than any of the Scottish regions, such as Cornwall, Merseyside and

several regions of Wales, all of which fell further behind in the
1980s (*Regional Trends* 29: 176–7). The over representation of
Scotland at Westminster in terms of the British population distribution is another likely target for reform. The Union may
face attack from a variety of directions in the near future, especially if the national economy continues to conceal the green
shoots of recovery.

A changing balance?

Dissatisfaction with the Union in Scotland has grown in the
twentieth century and especially in recent decades in conjunction with economic change and unemployment. The Union
cannot be blamed, legitimately, for the problems of the Scottish economy which are rooted in historical development and
common to other parts of the United Kingdom. But the success of the present government in resolving those problems
through economic management, or the possibility that a better
outcome might be achieved under an independent regime, provide valid criteria for judging the future economic usefulness
of the Union.

At present, the economic balance appears to favour the
status quo, which is certainly the safest option. The case for
independence is usually, and quite naturally, expounded in
optimistic terms. But success depends on all the hopeful
assumptions being fulfilled. New policies must generate substantial increases in employment, oil revenues must be sustained, and together they must close the gap between public
expenditure and taxation from which Scotland has benefited
throughout the present century. This would indeed be a
remarkable performance with no precedent in recent historical
experience. This optimistic prognosis for an independent econ-

omy tends to gloss over the weaknesses in the Scottish economy. The idea that Scotland is a strong economy being dragged down by a failing United Kingdom economy paints an attractive scenario for many in Scotland. But the fact is that while the United Kingdom is a weak and troubled economy, Scotland contains some of its more feeble constituent parts. The great advantage of the Union in these circumstances lies in the very substantial transfer payments from central government for social security and welfare on a scale well above the taxation revenue raised in Scotland. Devolution offers a potentially attractive middle way, less risky than independence but with more self-determination than the status quo. Whether such a system turned out to be a great success or an unmitigated disaster would depend, in large part, on the form it took especially with regard to the distribution of public expenditure gains and tax obligations. It is, thus, very difficult to predict the probable outcome of the adoption of devolution.

But no economic or political system remains unchanged, and the balance of advantage could swing away from the Union by a large increase in oil revenues from increased exploitation or a rise in price, or from a reduction in the gains from the revenue/expenditure account. The latter may be the more likely. The enduring difficulties of the United Kingdom economy, the inbuilt expansion of the social security component of the public sector finances, the accumulated effects of decades of failure to invest in infrastructure in transport, schools, hospitals and many other areas, together with the persistent weakness of the performance of trade and industry, all impose massive pressures on public sector expenditures and the level of taxation required to provide them. There is little evidence of consensus or, despite the posturing of politicians, much apparent enthusiasm to make hard choices. But the present administration clearly wishes to resolve the problem of the public sector deficit by reducing public spending. Success in this direction will almost certainly diminish the gain through transfer payments of regions, like Scotland, which currently enjoy more in expenditure than they contribute in revenue. As this benefit declines, so one of the principal economic advantages of the Union to Scotland will be diminished. Ironically, one of the main threats to the Union may come from the government of the party most firmly committed to it, and from the demands upon it of its natural constituency in southern England.

In the final analysis, the decision to support any of these alternatives will be determined by the majority of individuals on grounds which are not exclusively economic, and possibly without any economic consideration at all. While the balance of past economic benefits and costs from the Union is fairly clear, any future extrapolation is fraught with difficulty. It depends crucially upon the economic policies pursued by the United Kingdom or Scottish government which in turn would depend on the party in power, and upon the extent to which the movement towards European integration is resumed. In that case independence or union may not even matter economically if macroeconomic policy is largely determined at European Union level. What can be predicted with the greatest confidence is that the problems facing the Scottish economy for the rest of this century and in the early part of the next will be no easier than those which have cast such a shadow over most of the twentieth century, whatever political or economic structures are adopted to face them.

Bibliography

Abbreviations:

SAS: *Scottish Abstract of Statistics*
SEB: *Scottish Economic Bulletin*
RT: *Regional Trends*

Text References

Adams, Ian H. 1978. *The Making of Urban Scotland.* London.

Ashcroft, B. 1988. 'External Take-Overs and Scottish Manufacturing Industry: The Effect on Local Linkages and Corporate Functions', *Scottish Journal of Political Economy*, 35.

Ashcroft, B. K. and Love, J. H. 1989. 'Evaluating the Effects of External Take-Overs on the Performance of Regional Companies: The Case of Scotland 1965–80', *Environment Planning* A, 21.

Ashcroft, B. K. , Love, J. H., and Malloy, E. 1991. 'Firm Formation in the British Counties with Special Reference to Scotland', *Regional Studies*, 25.

Ashworth, William 1986. *The History of the British Coal Industry. Volume 5 1946–1982: The Nationalised Industry.* Oxford.

Atherton, Cynthia M. 1991. 'The Development of the Middle Class Suburb: The West End of Glasgow', *Scottish Economic and Social History*, 11.

Baird, Robert 1954. 'Local Government Finance' and 'Housing' in Cairncross, A. K. (ed) *The Scottish Economy*. Cambridge.

Baumol, William. 1967. 'The Macroeconomics of Unbalanced Growth', *American Economic Review*, 57.

Beesley, M. E. and Hamilton, R. T. 1986. 'Births and Deaths of Manufacturing Firms in the Scottish Regions', *Regional Studies*, 20.

Begg, Tom 1987. *50 Special Years: A Study in Scottish Housing*. London.

Bowen, Alex and Mayhew, Ken (eds) 1991. *Reducing Regional Inequalities*. London.

Breton, Albert 1974. *The Economic Theory of Representative Government*. London.

Brown, A. J. 1972. *The Framework of Regional Economics in Britain*. Cambridge.

Buchanan, J. M. and Tullock, G. 1962. *The Calculus of Consent*. Ann Arbor.

Butt, John. 1971. 'Working-Class Housing in Glasgow, 1851–1914', in Chapman, Stanley D. (ed) *The History of Working-Class Housing*. London.

Buxton, N. K. 1968. 'The Scottish Shipbuilding Industry between the Wars: A Comparative Study', *Business History*, 10.

Buxton, N. K. 1970. 'Entrepreneurial Efficiency in the British Coal Industry between the Wars', *Economic History Review*, 2nd ser. 23.

Buxton, N. K. 1976. 'Efficiency and Organisation in Scotland's Iron and Steel Industry during the Interwar Period', *Economic History Review*. 2nd ser. 29.

Buxton, N. K. 1980. 'Economic Growth in Scotland between the Wars: The Role of Production Structure and Rationalisation', *Economic History Review*, 2nd ser. 33.

Buxton, N. K. 1985. 'The Scottish Economy 1945–79: Performance, Structure and Problems', in Saville, R. (ed) *The Economic Development of Modern Scotland 1950–1980*. Edinburgh.

Cage, R. A. 1994. 'Infant Mortality Rates and Housing: Twentieth Century Glasgow', *Scottish Economic and Social History*, 14.

Campbell, A. D. 1954. 'Income', in Cairncross, A. K. (ed) *The Scottish Economy*. Cambridge.

Campbell, A. D. 1955. 'Changes in Scottish Incomes 1924–49', *Economic Journal*, 65.

Campbell, R. H. 1964. 'The Anglo-Scottish Union of 1707. II The Economic Consequences', *Economic History Review*, 2nd ser. 16.

Campbell, R. H. 1974. 'The Union and Economic Growth', in Rae, T. I. (ed) *The Union of 1707: Its Impact on Scotland*. Glasgow.

Campbell, R. H. 1978. 'The North British Locomotive Company between the Wars', *Business History*, 20.

Campbell, R. H. 1979. 'The Scottish Office and the Special Areas in the 1930s', *Historical Journal*, 22.

Campbell, R. H. 1980. *The Rise and Fall of Scottish Industry 1707–1939*. Edinburgh.

Cornford, J. P. and Brand, J. A. 1969. 'Scottish Voting Behaviour', in Wolfe, J. N. (ed) *Government and Nationalism in Scotland*. Edinburgh.

Craig, F. W. S. 1989. *British Electoral Facts 1832–1987*. London.

Cramond, R. D. 1966. *Housing Policy in Scotland 1919–1964; A Study in State Assistance*. Edinburgh.

Danson, M., Lloyd, M. G. and Newlands, D. 1989. 'Scottish Enterprise: Towards a Model Agency or a Flawed Initiative?', *Regional Studies*, 23.

Devine, T. M. 1975. *The Tobacco Lords*. Edinburgh.

Devine, T. M. 1985. 'The Union of 1707 and Scottish Development', *Scottish Economic and Social History*, 5.

Donaldson, G., Ferguson, W., Simpson, J. M., Bannerman, J. W. M. and Cowan, E. J. 'Scottish Devolution: The Historical Background', in Wolfe, J. N. (ed) *Government and Nationalism in Scotland*. Edinburgh.

Dow, Sheila. 1988. 'The Scottish Balance of Payments', *The Royal Bank of Scotland Review*, 160.

Dow, Sheila. 1992. 'The Regional Financial Sector: A Scottish Case Study', *Regional Studies*, 26.

Dunnett, Peter J. S. 1980. *The Decline of the British Motor Industry: the Effects of Government Policy, 1945–79*. London.

Durie, A. J. 1979. *The Scottish Linen Industry in the Eighteenth Century*. Edinburgh.

Feinstein, C. H. 1972. *Statistical Tables of National Income, Expenditure and Output of the UK 1855–1965*. Cambridge.

Ferguson, W. 1977. *Scotland's Relations with England: A Survey to*

1707. Edinburgh.

Finlay, Richard. J. 1994a. *Independent and Free: Scottish Politics and the Origins of the Scottish National Party 1918–1945*. Edinburgh.

Finlay, Richard. J. 1994b. 'National Identity in Crisis: Politicians, Intellectuals and the "End of Scotland" 1920–1939', (unpublished manuscript).

Firn, John R. and Roberts, David 1984. 'High-Technology Industries', in Hood, Neil and Young, Stephen (eds) *Industry, Policy and the Scottish Economy*. Edinburgh.

Gibb, Andrew. 1989. 'Policy and Politics in Scottish Housing since 1945', in Rodger, Richard (ed) *Scottish Housing in the Twentieth Century*. Leicester.

Hamilton, R. T. 1986. 'The Influence of Unemployment on the Level and Rate of Company Formation in Scotland 1950–1984'. *Environment and Planning* A, 18.

Harley, Knick 1994. 'Foreign Trade: Comparative Advantage and Performance', in Floud, Roderick and McCloskey, Donald (eds), *The Economic History of Britain since 1700: Volume 1: 1700–1860*. Cambridge.

Harris, A., Lloyd, M. G., McGuire, A. J. and Newlands, D. A. 1986. 'Who Gains from Structural Change? The Distribution of the Benefits of Oil in Aberdeen', *Urban Studies*, 23.

Harris, R. I. D. 1989. *The Growth and Structure of the UK Regional Economy 1963–85*. Aldershot.

Harvie, Christopher 1994. *Scotland and Nationalism: Scottish Society and Politics 1707–1994*. London.

Haug, Peter 1986. 'US High Technology Multinationals and Silicon Glen', *Regional Studies*, 20.

Hayton, K. 1992. 'The Decline of Public–Private Partnerships: The Fate of the Scottish Enterprise Trusts under Scottish Enterprise', *Regional Studies*, 26.

Heald, David 1990. '*Financing a Scottish Parliament: Options for Debate*', Scottish Foundation for Economic Research. Edinburgh.

Helm, Dieter and Smith, Stephen 1987. 'The Assessment: Decentralisation and the Economics of Local Government', *Oxford Review of Economic Policy*, 3.

Henderson, Jeffrey 1989. *The Globalisation of High Technology Pro-*

duction: *Society, Space and Semiconductors in the Restructuring of the Modern World*. London.

Hill, Stephen and Munday, Max 1992. 'The UK Regional Distribution of Foreign Direct Investment: Analysis and Determinants', *Regional Studies*, 26.

Hood, Neil. 1991. 'The Scottish Development Agency in Retrospect', *The Royal Bank of Scotland Review*, 171.

Hood, Neil and Young, Stephen (eds) 1984. *Industry, Policy and the Scottish Economy*. Edinburgh.

Hubley, John 1983. 'Poverty and Health in Scotland', in Brown, Gordon and Cook, Robin (eds) *Scotland: The Real Divide*. Edinburgh.

Hughes, Gordon A. 1987. 'Fiscal Federalism in the U. K.', *Oxford Review of Economic Policy*, 3.

Hume, J. R. and Moss, M. S. 1979. *Beardmore: The History of a Scottish Industrial Giant*. London.

Hutton, Will 'Ailing London is Net Contributor to Rest of UK', *Guardian*, 27 July 1993.

Jeremy, David J. 1991. 'The Hundred Largest Employers in the U. K.: 1907, 1935, 1955', *Business History*, 33.

Kay, J. A. and King, M. A. 1992. *The British Tax System*. Oxford.

Knox, William , McKinlay, Alan and Smyth, James 1993. 'Industrialisation, Work and Labour Politics: Clydeside, c. 1850–1990', in Schulze, Rainer (ed) *Industrieregionen im Umbruch*. Essen.

Law, Christopher M. 1980. *British Regional Development since World War 1*. London.

Lee, C. H. 1979. *British Regional Employment Statistics 1841–1971*. Cambridge.

Lee, C. H. 1983. 'Modern Economic Growth and Structural Change in Scotland: The Service Sector Reconsidered', *Scottish Economic and Social History*, 3.

Lee, C. H. 1986. *The British Economy since 1700: A Macroeconomic Perspective*. Cambridge.

Lee, C. H. 1991. 'Regional Inequalities in Infant Mortality in Britain, 1861–1971: Patterns and Hypotheses, *Population Studies*, 45.

Lenman, Bruce. 1977. *An Economic History of Modern Scotland 1660–1976*. London.

Leser, C. E. V. 1954. 'Coal-Mining' and 'Production', in Cairncross, A. K. *The Scottish Economy*. Cambridge.

Leser, C. E. V. and Silvey, A. H. 1950. 'Scottish Industries during the Inter-War Period', *Manchester School*, 18.

Levack, B. P. 1987. *The Formation of the British State*. Oxford.

Lever, William and Moore, Chris 1986. 'The City in Transition: Policies and Agencies for the Regeneration of Clydeside', in Hausner, Victor A. (ed) *Economic Change in British Cities*. Oxford.

Levitt, Ian 1983. 'Scottish Poverty: The Historical Background', in Brown, G. and Cook, R. *Scotland: The Real Divide*. Edinburgh.

Lorenz, Edward and Wilkinson, Frank 1986. 'The Shipbuilding Industry 1880–1965', in Elbaum, Bernard and Lazonick, William (eds) *The Decline of the British Economy*. Oxford.

Love, J. H. 1990. 'External Take-Over and Regional Linkage Adjustment: the Case of Scotch Whisky', *Environment and Planning* A, 22.

Lythe, C. and Majimudar, M. 1982. *The Renaissance of the Scottish Economy?* London.

McCrone, Gavin 1965. *Scotland's Economic Progress 1951–1960: A Study in Regional Accounting*. London.

McCrone, Gavin 1969. *Regional Policy in Britain*. London.

McCrone, Gavin 1985. 'The Role of Government', in Saville, Richard *The Economic Development of Modern Scotland*. Edinburgh.

MacKay, D. I. and Buxton, N. K. 1965. 'The North of Scotland Economy – A Case for Redevelopment?', *Scottish Journal of Political Economy*, 12.

MacKay, D. I. and Mackay, G. A. 1975. *The Political Economy of North Sea Oil*. London.

Mackay, Tony 1984. 'The Oil and Oil-Related Sector', in Hood, Neil and Young, Stephen (eds) *Industry, Policy and the Scottish Economy*. London.

Maclennan, Duncan, Gibb, Kenneth and More, Alison 1991. *Fairer Subsidies, Faster Growth: Housing, Government and the Economy*. London.

Marshall, J. N. *et al.* 1988. *Services and Uneven Development*. Oxford.

Martin, Ron 1989. 'The Political Economy of Britain's North-South Divide', in Lewis, Jim and Townsend, Alan (eds) *The North-South Divide: Regional Change in Britain in the 1980s*. London.

Midwinter, Arthur, Keating, Michael and Mitchell, James 1991. *Politics and Public Policy in Scotland*. London.

Mitchell, B. R. 1988. *British Historical Statistics*. Cambridge.

Moore, B., Rhodes, J. and Tyler, P. 1986. *The Effects of Government Regional Policy*. London.

Moore, B. and Rhodes, J. 1974. 'Regional Policy and the Scottish Economy', *Scottish Journal of Political Economy*, 21.

Oates, W. E. 1972. *Fiscal Federalism*. New York.

O'Farrell, P. N., Hitchens, D. M. W. N. and Moffat, L. A. R. 1992. 'Competitiveness of Business Service Firms: A Matched Comparison between Scotland and the South East of England', *Regional Studies*, 26.

Pacione, M. 1986. 'Quality of Life in Glasgow: An Applied Geographical Analysis', *Environment and Planning* A, 18.

Pagnamenta, Peter and Overy, Richard. 1984. *All Our Working Lives*. London.

Parsons, Wayne. 1988. *The Political Economy of British Regional Policy*. London.

Payne, Peter. L. 1979. *Colvilles and the Scottish Steel Industry*. Oxford.

Payne, Peter. L. 1985. 'The Decline of the Scottish Heavy Industries 1945–1983', in Saville, Richard (ed) *The Economic Development of Modern Scotland*. Edinburgh.

Payne, Peter L. 1988. *The Hydro*. Aberdeen.

Payne, Peter L. 1992. *Growth and Contraction: Scottish Industry c1860–1990*, Studies in Scottish Economic and Social History, 2.

Peacock, Alan T. and Wiseman, Jack 1967. *The Growth of Public Expenditure in the United Kingdom*. London.

Peebles, Hugh B. 1987. *Warshipbuilding on the Clyde: Naval Orders and the Prosperity of the Clyde Shipbuilding Industry, 1889–1939*. Edinburgh.

Pike, W. J. 1993. 'The Oil Price Crisis and its Impact on Scottish North Sea Development 1986–1988', *Scottish Economic and Social History*, 13.

Pollard, S. 1982. *The Wasting of the British Economy: British Economic Policy 1945 to the Present*. London.

Pollard, S. and Robertson, Paul 1979. *The British Shipbuilding Industry 1870–1914*. Cambridge, Mass.

Price, Sylvia 1981. 'Rivetters' Earnings in Clyde Shipbuilding 1889–1913', *Scottish Economic and Social History*, 1.

Rodger, Richard. 1986. 'The Victorian Building Industry and the Housing of the Scottish Working Class', in: Doughty, Martin (ed), *Building the Industrial City*. Leicester.

Rodger, Richard 1989. 'Crisis and Confrontation in Scottish Housing 1880–1914', in Rodger, Richard (ed) *Scottish Housing in the Twentieth Century*. Leicester.

Rodger, Richard and Al-Qaddo, Hunain 1989. 'The Scottish Special Housing Association and the Implementation of Housing Policy 1937–87', in Rodger, Richard (ed) *Scottish Housing in the Twentieth Century*. Leicester.

Rosie, George 1992. '*Scotching the Myth*', Scottish Centre for Economic and Social Research, 17. Peterhead.

Routh, G. 1980. *Occupation and Pay in Great Britain 1906–1979*. Glasgow.

Rubinstein, W. D. 1987. *Elites and the Wealthy in Modern British History*. Brighton.

Salmond, Alex 1993. *Horizons without Bars: The Future of Scotland*. Edinburgh.

Sandford, C. 1992. *Economics of Public Finance*. Oxford.

Saville, Richard (ed) 1985. *The Economic Development of Modern Scotland 1950–1980*. Edinburgh.

Scott, J. and Hughes, M. 1980. *The Anatomy of Scottish Capital*. London.

Scottish Centre for Economic and Social Research. 31 March 1992. *Static Scottish Budget 1991/92*. Peterhead.

Scottish National Party 1993. *The Scottish Budget for an Independent Parliament: Towards a Prosperous Scotland*. Edinburgh.

Short, J. 1981. *Public Expenditure and Taxation in UK Regions*. Farnborough.

Simpson, David 1963. 'Investment, Employment and Government Expenditure in the Highlands 1951–1960', *Scottish Journal of Polit-*

ical Economy, 10.

Slaven, A. 1975. *The Development of the West of Scotland*. London.

Slaven, A. 1977. 'A Shipyard in Depression: John Browns of Clydebank 1919–1938', *Business History*, 19.

Slaven, A. 1982. 'Management and Shipbuilding, 1890–1938: Structure and Strategy in the Shipbuilding Firm on the Clyde', in Slaven, Anthony and Aldcroft, Derek H. (eds) *Business, Banking and Urban History*. Edinburgh.

Smith, R. 1979. *East Kilbride: The Biography of a Scottish New Town, 1947–1973*. London.

Smith, Roger and Farmer, Elspeth 'Housing, Population and Decentralisation', In Smith, Roger and Wannup, Urlan (eds) 1985. *Strategic Planning in Action: The Impact of the Cylde Valley Regional Plan 1946–1982*. Aldershot.

Smout, T. C. 1964. 'The Anglo-Scottish Union of 1707. I The Economic Background', *Economic History Review*, 2nd ser. 16.

Southall, Humphrey R. 1988. 'The Origins of the Depressed Areas: Unemployment, Growth and Regional Economic Structure in Britain before 1914', *Economic History Review*, 2nd ser. 41.

Storey, D. J. and Johnson, S. 1987. 'Regional Variations in Entrepreneurship in the UK', *Scottish Journal of Political Economy*, 34.

Strath, Bo 1987. *The Politics of De-Industrialisation: The Contraction of the West European Shipbuilding Industry*. London.

Supple, Barry 1987. *The History of the British Coal Industry. 4. 1913–1946: The Political Economy of Decline*. Oxford.

Swales, J. K. 1983. 'Industrial Policy in Scotland', in Ingham, Keith P. D. and Love, James (eds) *Understanding the Scottish Economy*. Oxford.

Tolliday, Steven 1987. *Business, Banking and Politics: The Case of British Steel 1918–1939*. Cambridge, Mass.

Tomkins, J. and Twomey, J. 1990. 'The Changing Spatial Structure of Manufacturing Plant in Great Britain 1976 to 1987', *Environment and Planning* A, 22.

Tomlinson, Jim 1994. 'British Economic Policy since 1945', in Floud, Roderick and McCloskey, Donald (eds) *The Economic History of Britain since 1700: Volume 3: 1939–1992*. Cambridge.

Treble, J. H. 1979. *Urban Poverty in Britain 1830–1914*. London.

Treble, J. H. 1980. 'The Pattern of Investment of the Standard Life Assurance Company 1875–1914', *Business History*, 22.

Trotman-Dickenson, D. I. 1961. 'The Scottish Industrial Estates', *Scottish Journal of Political Economy*, 8.

Turok, I. 1992. 'Developing Skills, Securing Jobs? Evaluating an Integrated Local Employment Initiative', *Regional Studies*, 26.

Turok, I. and Richardson, P. 1991. 'New Firms and Local Economic Development: Evidence from West Lothian', *Regional Studies*, 25.

Twomey, J. and Taylor, J. 1985. 'Regional Policy and the Interregional Movement of Manufacturing Industry in Great Britain', *Scottish Journal of Political Economy*, 32.

Veverka, J. 1963. 'The Growth of Government Expenditure in the United Kingdom since 1790', *Scottish Journal of Political Economy*, 10.

Wardley, Peter 1991. 'The Anatomy of Big Business; Aspects of Corporate Development in the Twentieth Century', *Business History*, 33.

Weir, Ron 1989. 'Rationalisation and Diversification in the Scotch Whisky Industry, 1900–1939: Another Look at "Old" and "New" Industries', *Economic History Review*, 2nd ser. 42.

Whatley, C. A. 1989. 'Economic Causes and Consequences of the Union of 1707: A Survey', *Scottish Historical Review*, 68.

Whatley, C. A. 1994. *Bought and Sold for English Gold?: Explaining the Union of 1707*, Studies in Scottish Economic and Social History, 4.

Wilks, Stephen 1988. *Industrial Policy and the Motor Industry*. Manchester.

Young, Stephen 1984. 'The Foreign-Owned Manufacturing Sector', in Hood, Neil and Young, Stephen (eds) *Industry, Policy and the Scottish Economy*. London.

Government Publications

Cmd 2353: Report of the Royal Commission on Coal Supplies, 1905.

Cmd 8731: Royal Commission on the Housing of the Industrial Population of Scotland Rural and Urban, 1917.

Cmd 6171: Royal Commission on the Distribution of Income and Wealth, Report No 1, 1975.

Cmd 2225: Scotland in the Union: A Partnership for Good. Edinburgh, 1993.

Industry Department for Scotland. 1988. *Scottish Enterprise: A New Approach to Training and Enterprise Creation.*

Report from Scottish Affairs Committee, Highlands and Islands Development Board, 1985.

Scottish Office, *Scottish Abstract of Statistics.* (various years).

Scottish Office, *Scottish Economic Bulletin.* (various years).

Central Statistical Office, *Regional Trends.* (various years).

Index